BREAKING BARRIERS

BREAKING BARRIERS

The Story of a Liberal Muslim Woman's Passage in Indian Politics

NAFEES FAZAL
with Sandhya Mendonca

KONARK

Konark Publishers Pvt. Ltd
New Delhi

Konark Publishers Pvt. Ltd
206, First Floor,
Peacock Lane, Shahpur Jat,
New Delhi 110 049
Phone: +91-11-41055065
e-mail: india@konarkpublishers.com, us@konarkpublishers.com
website: www.konarkpublishers.com

The photographs used in this book are from the author's collection.

ISBN: 978-81-956786-8-6

Edited by Ranjana Narayan
Cover Design by Sanjay Mathpal
Typeset by Saanvi Graphics, Noida
Printed and bound at Thomson Press (India) Ltd

This book is dedicated
in the name of God,
the most merciful,
and
to my loving and supportive family.

Contents

Foreword

CHANGE IS THE elixir of the future. In a country as young demographically as India, it is important to identify and empower change agents, so that their influence and their example spread throughout society. Nafees Fazal has from the start of her career in politics defined change, and defied conservatism and resistance to change. This was why my task was to ensure that Nafees was given an opportunity to work in the legislature and in the government, thereby leading by example. Hers has been a long and hard path, as may be expected from any individual who challenges the traditionalists. She stood up for gender equality, but this was not to the liking of several leaders, including many from the community to which she proudly belongs.

During the period when Nafees Fazal entered the political arena, she was almost alone among those of her faith and as a woman. It was a struggle to overcome prejudice, one that has been documented in her account of the past. While I was Chief Minister, Bengaluru was transformed into the IT hub of India and adopted international standards; and as External Affairs Minister, my effort was to instil within the Ministry of External Affairs, the verity that business is the lifeblood of the nation. It is an intrinsic part of foreign policy to seek to improve the economic standing of our country and its people. In all such tasks, it was essential to discover and place in positions of responsibility those capable of working, not with an obsession towards the past but a gaze into the future. Nafees was among those choices, and it must be added that her family and herself became close to our family, especially my wife Prema, and our children. Differences of faith bothered us not at all, and this is the strength of India.

During the freedom struggle, women, who were in the workforce as well as those who were sheltered in the cool recesses of highly traditional homesteads, found the courage to come out on the streets to demand that their children and their country shake off the yoke of foreign rule. After Independence, our sisters came out to create a better India. This is the story of one such person, and it is told in the frankness customary of Nafees.

Nafees Fazal epitomises the change in our country and the world. Born in a conservative Muslim family, with no real economic need to work for a living, Nafees chose to willingly enter the hurly-burly of politics. Married to the always supportive Hassan Fazal, she is the mother of two independent daughters. Nafees took her philosophy of nurturing and mentoring others, hard work and transparency into her political career as well as when she was appointed Karnataka's Minister of Medical Education in my cabinet.

This book is a study on the struggles and triumphs of a woman who has broken conventions and social taboos to live a life of service and fullness.

S.M. Krishna

Former External Affairs Minister &

Former Chief Minister, Karnataka

Advance Praise

It was 1979. They were hectic days—Devraj Urs had split with Indira Gandhi and was fighting the Lok Sabha elections in Karnataka under the banner of Congress (Urs). I was expecting my youngest child and out of the campaign, staying in my parents' home in Bangalore.

And there one morning, walked in a young glamorous Muslim girl, who introduced herself and said she had come for my advice. 'On what?' I asked her. 'On whether I should go to Congress(U) or stay with Indira*ji*.' I explained the situation as it was and she left, thanking me for being so frank. That was Nafees Fazal, the fearless firebrand young woman who decided to stay in Congress(I) and went on to become MLC and Minister, besides holding many other positions. This is her story – frank, daring, and gripping, and as only she can tell.

I have watched her, advised her, supported her, and at times admonished her. But I have admired her for what she is – an educated, bold, non-conventional Muslim woman, who has lived life on her terms and been willing to pay the price for it...

God bless her...

Margaret Alva
Former Union Minister and Former Governor

Nafees Fazal is a most unorthodox, unconventional person who has lived her whole life on her own principles and understanding of what values to uphold and which ones to reject. In other words, the perfect Indian woman for the 21st century. Her autobiography will make us all realise why she is a role model to be emulated. She has had her successes and her setbacks but has remained unfazed by all she has undergone. Her life is a MUST for all to study. I am privileged to have known her.

Mani Shankar Aiyar
Former MP (LS and RS) &
Former Union Minister

Ms Nafees Fazal has had an extraordinary life, a life of firm determination, independent views, and public service. Over a 40 year political career, she has stood up for individual liberty, opposed unjust laws, and served with distinction as a Minister in Karnataka. A rebel throughout her life, her story is a saga of courage and an inspiration for all of us.

T.V. Mohandas Pai
Chairman, Manipal Global Education & Aarin Capital

I have known Nafees Fazal for over four decades as a feisty politician who battled gender barriers to gain her rightful place in a male dominated bastion as one among equals.

Kiran Mazumdar-Shaw
Chairperson and Managing Director, Biocon

Nafees Fazal represents the New Indian Woman, who treasures her independence and carries none of the hangovers of the past when women were regarded in society as less than equal to men. Her courage and fighting spirit caused her and her loved ones some pain, but in the end, Nafees Fazal's example of modernity and fight against obsolete ways of thought inspired many women to follow in her wake, whatever be the faith they belonged to. The book is essential reading to understand from the inside what had gone wrong in the politics of India, and how a few spirited women fought against the odds to anchor India's polity in the needs and realities of the time.

Prof. Madhav Das Nalapat
UNESCO Peace Chair, Manipal University

Nafees Fazal is an example of loyalty and courage. She worked night and day joining the dedicated few who saw S.M. Krishna as the answer to the needs and problems of Karnataka. A facet of her vivid personality that shines out is the fact that Nafees never distinguishes on the basis of faith or region. She is Indian and proud of it, just as we as Indians are proud of her.

Lakshmi Bayi
Poet and writer

Smt. Nafees Fazal has been a client of mine for quite some time. She is intelligent, witty, and has a razor-sharp mind. She is able to analyse legal problems in a logical manner, befitting that of any lawyer. She shares liberal views and has a modern outlook. Even in the cabinet of Chief Minister S.M. Krishna, she was extremely efficient in the discharge of her duties as a Minister and had earned the encomium of the general public.

Udaya Holla
Senior Advocate &
Former Advocate General of Karnataka

Acknowledgements

This book would not have been possible without the unconditional love and support of my younger daughter Nooraine Fazal and my sonny Jitu Virwani.

I CAN'T THANK enough my dear husband Hassan for his constant and unwavering love and support. I cherish the joy that he, our eldest daughter Nishi and son-in-law Rafiq, grandsons Shariq and Ryaan, brothers Ameen Rahaman, Jameel Shacoor, Samad Motiwala, Irfan Razack, my daughter Nooraine and our friends bring to my life.

I would also like to acknowledge the encouragement and support that I have received in my political career from Margaret Alva, Prema and S.M. Krishna, Ambika Soni, R.K. Dhawan, Mani Shankar Aiyar, Louise and Salman Khurshid, Vincent George, Ghulam Nabi Azad, D.K. Shivakumar, R.V. Deshpande, and Janardhana Poojary.

I'm extremely grateful to former Principal Secretaries Tanga Raj, Shankarlinge Gowda and A.K.M. Naik, former Chief Secretaries S.V. Ranganath and Teresa Bhattacharya, Private Secretary Mirza

Akbarulla, Former Vice-Chancellor RGUHS Dr P.S. Prabhakaran, and my doctors Ranga Naik (cardiologist) K.G. Das (general physician) Dhiraj (gastroenterologist), Satish (pulmonologist), and Devi Shetty (heart surgeon, philanthropist and Padma Bhushan awardee).

It was Nooraine and one of her closest friends Divya Balagopal, who I consider another daughter who encouraged me to write the story of my life. They hoped that telling my story would be therapeutic for me, and be an inspiration and great learning for other women to become pathbreakers.

I especially wish to acknowledge my co-author Sandhya Mendonca for getting under my skin and articulating my story. I have enjoyed working with her on this book and am thankful to her.

M.D. 'Monu' Nalapat has been a catalyst in this project and I thank him for his insight and advice. I am delighted that Mr K.P.R. Nair agreed to publish my book and I acknowledge the support of all the people at Konark Publishers.

Nafees Fazal

Former Minister & Member of the Legislative Council, Karnataka

Introduction
Taqdeer & Takbeer

All of life is determined by Taqdeer & Takbeer.
One is the destiny written for you,
the other is the life you script for yourself.

NAFEES FAZAL REBELS against convention. She was the first Muslim woman to become a minister in Karnataka and in all of south India in 1999. Viewed through a contemporary lens, she is a prime example of a modern, articulate and focused woman. Unapologetically ambitious, she makes no bones about speaking her mind and pursuing what she wants.

The going was never easy when she stepped into politics at the fag end of the 1970s. Gender and religion shackled her: how a woman should behave, how a woman should behave in politics, how a Muslim woman should behave. When stumbling blocks kept popping up, Nafees dug her heels in and refused to buckle. Her sense of identity and self-awareness were non-negotiable. Scarred by childhood emotional traumas, her survival instinct was strong. Add to it a visceral self-belief that made her steadfast in her pursuit of self-actualisation. Dream, Visualise, Realise are her *mantras*.

Her personality is compelling. A husky voice and fashionable dress sense make heads turn. She has not underplayed her charismatic femininity and also refused to play the hypocritical game of 'dressing down' in Indian politics. The glamorous facade goes hand-in-hand with a razor-sharp mind. Self-taught and articulate, she was a quick learner and grasped the essence of the important portfolios she handled – Medical Education and Science & Technology. She initiated innovative projects that were far ahead of their time and gave Karnataka an edge early on.

Being a homemaker and society hostess were always easy options in the upper crust world that she inhabited, but the life of an appendage was not for her. She was too much of an individualist and chose to follow her career in politics. And what a roller coaster ride it took her on: there were dismal depths and dizzying highs, and long years of hard slog. She rubbed shoulders with the most powerful in the land and stood in the dock with criminals.

Her best friends say that Nafees is headstrong and not one to dissemble; she says what she thinks without a filter. This isn't a trait that fetches rewards, and what could have been hers eluded her. It's been 17 long years since she was a minister and over 19 years since she was a legislator. Now the shadows grow longer, and she looks back with a mix of anger and regret. For the opportunities that didn't come her way. At the obstacles that tripped her up.

The crowds don't throng No. 31, Viviani Road, as they once did. The aura of power isn't the same for an ex-minister and ex-legislator. Yearning and disappointment simmer just below the surface. The presence of a loving family and friends offers a little balm. A people's person, warm-hearted and generous, she draws energy from being amidst a flock, with the spotlight on her.

Age, however, hasn't mellowed her; on the contrary, it has given her the time to tell her story, warts and all. As in life, so in politics, a woman has it tough. Affluence, education, and connections don't make it easier. Politics is a power game in which men want to call the shots, and an assertive woman has her work cut out for her.

Nafees Fazal relates her life story the way she has lived life – no holds barred. Perhaps readers will find inspiration to be themselves, find their own identities and live their lives to the fullest.

—Sandhya Mendonca

Nafees Fazal, her husband Hassan (right) and her younger daughter Nooraine (left) with Margaret Alva (second from right), S.M. Krishna (third from right) and Prema Krishna (second from left) during the Eid celebration at their house in Bengaluru.

The manicured lawns of No 31, Viviani Road in the erstwhile Cantonment area of Bengaluru are a verdant green. This is where Nafees hosts well-attended parties on Ramzan and Eid al-Adha. Tasteful, white covered tables beckon invitingly under canopies, and tempting aromas waft from chafing dishes bearing festive delicacies. She is the perfect host, charming and radiant in a deep pink sari. Nafees Fazal is in her element as she adroitly weaves in and out of conversations, never letting the ball drop or a guest left unattended.

An unaware onlooker would not know from the grace and ease of her manner that amongst those present are the wealthiest and most powerful people in the state. She speaks to her adoring and attentive staff in the same manner and style that she speaks to her guests. Her manner in public and private, with everybody, is warm, considerate, and genuine. All along though, her keen senses are absorbing information, her brain ticking, sorting, and storing information. She's up to date with current events, and apart from being on top of political activities across the world, she follows sports especially tennis and cricket. Federer and Dhoni are her favourite sportspersons and she doesn't miss a single game that they play.

1

A Lot of Drama & Trauma

IF I'M FEISTY, and what you millennials call 'badass', let me tell you that I have always been like this. I don't mince my words and I don't take any nonsense from anyone, especially from men. To know why, we have to go back to my childhood.

I was amongst the fortunate few of my generation who were born free citizens of a new nation. I was born on 4 November 1947, just three months after India shook off the shackles of colonial rule. There had been bloody clashes during the painful partition of the country into India and Pakistan. That did not affect our family, well-secured by geography and wealth in south India.

My father, Abdul Kareem Rehman, was a good-looking man but an out-and-out philanderer. He owned areca nut plantations in Mettupalayam, in Coimbatore district of Tamil Nadu. In those days, the areca crop was like gold and it made him wealthy. The good things I remember of him are that he was well-educated, having studied at the Aligarh Muslim University. He was a voracious reader, and I remember him often reading until three in the morning. He sparked my interest in reading and current affairs as he used to read *The Illustrated Weekly*. When I was still in school, he would teach me about business and investments. I think I got my shrewdness and business acumen from him. Though I married young and went to college for just a year, I have been smart enough to educate myself.

Like any little girl, I was thrilled when I had his attention. But I had a difficult relationship with him, for though he could be loving at times, he was also cruel and downright sadistic. Daddy was a terrible husband, and forced me, a helpless child, and my younger siblings, to witness his abuse of our mother.

Plantations don't require round-the-year supervision. When the season was over, off went daddy on his philandering jaunts. We saw nothing of him for months on end. At times we would hear of his outings with some woman or the other. Daddy made plenty of money, bought several estates, and invested in many properties in Chennai and Mysuru. While he lavished money on his girlfriends, he kept mother on a tight budget. His desertion and stream of affairs caused my mother much anguish and she wept bitterly when he was away. But they were nothing compared to the tears she shed when he did come home.

What's inexplicable to me, even today, is why daddy made me watch their fights. He used to place me in a chair and seemed to revel in the fact that I was a captive spectator of their ugly exchanges. He used to shout insults and taunt mother, and when she retaliated, it unleashed more cruelty in him and increased the physical and verbal abuse he inflicted on her. In my innocence, I used to think that if only she kept quiet, he wouldn't behave so badly. Little did I know then of the nature of sadists and bullies, and that keeping silent would not appease them.

My mother Rukhiya was a bubbly, vivacious young scholar from Presentation Convent, Madras. She excelled in extra-curricular activities and played tennis. But her husband's neglect and abusive behaviour drove her to despair. Daddy's sister-in-law (his elder brother's wife) added fuel to the fire by spreading tales that he had married another woman. Rendered powerless and driven out of her mind, she threatened to jump into the well. I watched, frozen with fear. Instead of the reassurance, attention, and love that she craved, she was given electroconvulsive therapy (ECT).

Heartbroken and disgusted, I wanted to be anywhere but home. I used to flee to my maternal grandparents' home in Madras at every opportunity. Khan Bahadur Mohammed Moosa Sait, my *nana*, was a reputed businessman, a philanthropist, and a pillar of society. He had been the Sheriff of Madras* and was a leader of the community. *Nana* and *nani* pampered me and coddled me with affection. I could go to Spencer's in a chauffeur-driven car; with a purse full of money, I could shop for everything I wished to have.

I had all the material things but not peace or security. In the eyes of the world, Moosa Sait was a great role model. But he treated everyone at home very badly, and especially the women of the house who he controlled rigidly. I often saw him scold and slap my *nani*, Halimabai. I was the only one whom he spared and pampered as his precious princess.

I have seen many men like my father and grandfather, the public and private faces like Jekyll & Hyde; the uncle who used to burn my aunt's stomach with cigarette butts, the wife beaters, and the dysfunctional families they create. Regarded as worthless, the women

---

* An apolitical titular position of authority bestowed for one year on a prominent citizen of Madras. This post was abolished in 1998.

are empty shells, with all the energy and life sucked out of them. I resolved when I was very young that I would not allow it to happen to me. I have never allowed a man to get the better of me.

Abuse of any kind—physical, verbal, sexual, emotional—is unforgivable. I wouldn't wish any child to go through the emotional trauma that I went through. It was psychologically distressing to see my mother abused. Somewhere deep within me, distrust and hatred of men started to form.

As a survivor of emotional abuse, my advice to anyone in a bad marriage is: don't stay in a bad marriage for the sake of the children. It's better to go your separate ways but try to stay friends for the sake of the children.

Daddy gave up drinking and womanising from 1957, after he went on the Haj (pilgrimage to Mecca) but he still continued his physical abuse of mummy till the day he died of a cardiac arrest at the age of 59.

Abandoned at the Gate

My life was filled with stress and fear from an early age. At one point, daddy felt we were getting spoiled by my grandparents and packed me and my younger brother, Ameen, to boarding school. The Lawrence School is in Lovedale, situated high up in the Nilgiris mountain range, near the popular hill station of Ooty.

I set off to school reluctantly but fashionably. When *nana* asked me what I wanted as a going-away gift, I asked for a hair perm. He died a month later, and I learnt of this only three months later, when I came home for the winter break.

Ameen was six and I was seven and being sent away to school seemed like banishment. What do kids know of the workings of an adult mind? Until then, we had never been separated from the family and the security of home. Mummy tried but couldn't change daddy's mind. As my parents drove away from the school yard, Ameen and I ran after them, holding on to the bumper of their Fiat desperately. I can still feel the ache of that painful separation. Mummy was devastated on parting from her children; you can imagine the pain a mother goes through. She was heartbroken and traumatised.

Being separated from my family left a deep scar on my mind. I realised the emotional damage the parting caused me much later, as the fear of abandonment stayed with me. Some years later, my parents moved me to a girls' only school, the Sacred Heart, in Yercaud (a hill station in Tamil Nadu).

Unable to control anything that was happening around me and to me, I began to rebel against everything. I always fought to get my own way, and became overly assertive and cheeky, at school and at home. When I didn't get selected for the school debates or elocutions, I staged sit-ins. I did make some good friends at school: Teresa Bhattacharya (*nee* Abraham) was my senior; she joined the IAS and rose to the rank of the chief secretary of Karnataka, and Jennifer Arul, media maven, who has remained one of my closest friends.

Some scars are invisible, and they fester, never fading. My emotional scars have shaped my persona. Looking back, I can't pick one bad spot; my early years seem to be a series of bad patches. They moulded my personality; I learnt to conceal my soft heart, and when scorned or hurt, I became a person who would exact an eye for an eye and a tooth for a tooth.

Sibling Rivalry

I was the eldest of four children; after me were Ameen, Nadira and our youngest brother, Mathin. Nobody who met me in later years would believe it but I suffered from an inferiority complex. When I was young, I was always roly-poly, while Nadira, my younger sister, was like a delicate doll.

All the people we knew constantly complimented Nadira who was indeed a radiant beauty. Although no one said anything uncomplimentary to me, the constant refrain of 'Nadira is so beautiful' used to make me feel plain in comparison. I was eight when I first began to feel a sense of inadequacy and my sibling became a rival.

How cruel adults are – intentionally or unintentionally. It's a terrible thing to do to any little child, to make them feel less appreciated and less loved. It leads to self-doubt, lack of self-esteem, and the loosening of bonds between siblings – creating dislike and disharmony. How can a young child articulate such feelings? Feeling like a plain Jane added yet another chip on my shoulder.

Luckily, I had a very perceptive uncle, my father's younger brother Omer Rehman who lived at home with us. His piercing eyes didn't miss a beat and he picked up my lack of confidence on my visits home from the boarding school. He told me, 'Baby, you are like Rita Hayworth.' I didn't know then that she was a glamorous Hollywood actor, but I could understand that he meant it as a compliment.

It was a much-needed boost for an insecure teenager, and it made me realise that I had my share of good looks. I can't tell you how good it made me feel and I think it created the persona you see today. How little do we realise the power of kind words!

Bad Touch

Another uncle was not a nice person; he was a sexual predator who put me through a traumatic experience by touching me inappropriately. This happened in Chennai when I was much younger. My grandfather had passed away and I was visiting my grandmother; at some point, I was alone with this man, a family member, who molested me. It was a horrible experience. A child can make out a good touch from bad touch. I was a spunky young girl but because I didn't know how to handle it, I didn't tell anybody in the family. I was lucky that he stopped at just touching me inappropriately but the experience added to the emotional scars I was carrying. It added to my mistrust of men, and I still carry residual anger against them.

To the outside world, there was nothing lacking in my life as they could only see that I was born privileged and pampered. But within the four walls of our home, it was a dismal story. I haven't written all this to seek your sympathy but to lay my life open so you can see that appearances are deceptive. Life isn't easy, for anyone.

Romance in the Garden City

To be the object of someone's love is a wonderful thing. But when Hassan began wooing me, I was unprepared. I was still in my teens, and just out of high school. I used to visit my uncle quite often in Bengaluru and I was having fun, away from the hell that was my parents' home.

The Fazals owned an upmarket clothing store on Commercial Street; the store was one of a kind and the family was renowned. They lived quite close to my uncle's house and Hassan was the gawky eldest son of the Fazals. He seemed to be besotted with me as soon as he saw me and began a typical 'filmi' style wooing, following me on his Lambretta scooter. I was annoyed by his attention as I was not interested in romance. Though I realised it only later, the behaviour of the only men I knew well until then – grandfather, daddy, and the bad uncle – had put me off the entire male gender.

My passion lay elsewhere. When I was 13 years old, I decided that I would enter politics. It was a photo of the beautiful and elegant young Indira Gandhi with her father, Prime Minister Jawaharlal Nehru, which prompted that decision. The photographs of Indira with her father Pandit Nehru depicted the close bond between father and daughter. I made up my mind that if I couldn't have a similar relationship with my father, then I would at least be strong and confident like Indira if I could enter politics. It was a dream that never died, despite all the upheaval and tumult in my life.

When Hassan was wooing me, it was a lopsided courtship as I wasn't swept off my feet. When he proposed to me, I told him that we could be friends or like brother and sister as I really didn't see us being together. I told him more than once that we were a mismatch. Hassan wore thick glasses which I used to mock by calling him a 'four-eyed gunner'. Despite my callous behaviour, he persisted with his attention and gently and slowly won me over. During our courtship, he did everything I asked: he took me dancing at the Catholic Club, and learned to eat Chinese food because I love it. It seems silly now even for a 16-year-old to make such demands but Hassan, who was 22, happily agreed to my whims.

I told him about my dream of entering politics and he agreed to support me. I was impressed by his kindness, his determination to make it in business, and his strength of character. My mother had begun to look for alliances for me, and she felt that Hassan was the best choice.

When we got around to informing the other family members, daddy threw a spanner in the works. He had diversified his business and had set up a gears and pinions business to manufacture bevel gears, in collaboration with a Russian partner. He wanted me to marry an educated guy, a professional settled in America.

But mummy was adamant about supporting my decision and Hassan won daddy over with his charm. We got married in December 1964 when I was 17, and he's been the perfect husband to me, and the best father to our two daughters, our rock-solid strength and support. I struck it lucky when I chose Hassan as my life partner!

Onions Make You Cry

As a young bride, I moved into the joint family of the Fazals. Hassan was madly in love with me, but marriage wasn't exactly a bed of roses. After the wedding, I went back to studies as I wanted to complete my graduation, but I was forced to cut it short after a year. I also wanted to learn Bharatanatyam but was told it was not for girls from 'good' families. Like many people of his generation, my father thought that it was only for courtesans. Wishing to study further and learn classical dance were simple wants, yet they were denied to me.

There were far more important things that I had to deal with, like a rolling-pin-wielding mother-in-law. I'm not joking; Hajra Fazal was a hard taskmaster and treated me like a maid. Those years there was water scarcity in Bengaluru and she would wake me up at dawn to fill buckets of water. Hassan's younger brother had a dog, Silver, and she would make me clean the dog's kennel.

Having led a pampered life at home and in boarding school, these chores were a shock. My mother had tried to train me to be a homemaker. She used to make me slice 30 onions a day, and tears would stream down my cheeks. I was very angry when she tried to teach me to cook. Her training had seemed regimental. Later in life, I began to enjoy it and became an excellent cook.

But as a new bride, my mother's attempts to teach me seemed like a piece of cake compared to what my dear mother-in-law had in store for me. She was a banshee who frightened and beat everybody, family, and staff. I still have nightmares about one incident in particular. One year during Ramzan, while we were preparing for the *iftar,* she asked me to cook for 50 people who worked at the store. When I said I couldn't do it, she came at me with a rolling pin and clobbered me. My elder daughter Nishi, who was still a little child, flung herself over me to protect me. She remembers this incident to date with horror.

Things didn't get better as time passed, and I seemed to be living in a madhouse. Hassan, who was my supporter in all other matters, refused to take sides. 'Even if you want to kill each other, don't involve me. Keep me out,' he said when either of us went to him with complaints against the other. He also teased me that this would be good training for the life in politics that I hankered after. I managed to move my family out to a bungalow in the neighbourhood, when my brother-in-law got married in 1969. We have been living peacefully here in 'Gulistan', our home which we subsequently bought from my grandfather's trust in the early 2000s.

All through these years, my dream had stayed alive. I reminded Hassan that I had agreed to marry him on the condition that he wouldn't curb my ambitions. He had asked then that I hold off for a few years. But now I was 30 years old, and the clock was ticking. I had given my undivided attention to the family for 13 years. It was time for me to step out into the sunshine.

As in any contract, one must enter marriage with openness and clear understanding. Before we got married, I was frank with Hassan about my political ambitions and we negotiated that I would give the early years to our family after which, I would pursue my political career. I fulfilled my commitment and Hassan fulfilled his. Despite all our challenges, and the times when our personal and professional lives were not aligned, our marriage has stood the test of time because it was based on truth. I can't empathise with today's generation which has no patience with their life partners. They fight with each other at the drop of a hat and want a divorce. Hassan and I are together even after 58 years despite the ups and downs of life.

2

Plunging into Politics: Thrills, Misses & Hits

I IDOLIZED INDIRA Gandhi through my teens, but I never imagined that one day I would be able to meet and interact with her and be acknowledged by her for my work within the Congress party.

But let me start at the beginning when I almost joined the wrong Congress! Sometimes I look back and wonder at my naïveté. But back in 1979, I was just shaking off the shackles of being a housewife. I had lived in a domesticated cocoon and had no idea how to go about establishing my own identity in politics. I turned to a powerful family friend for advice and help.

Azeez Sait *chacha* was a politician from Mysuru and was known as the stormy petrel of Karnataka politics. He was the first Muslim member of the State Legislative Council and was a legislator for an uninterrupted tenure of 18 years and held several portfolios as a minister. Sait was as courteous as ever when I told him, '*Chacha*, I want to join politics.' He thought it best that I take the advice of another woman politician and he suggested that I meet Mrs Margaret Alva.

Margaret*ji* was a Member of Parliament (Rajya Sabha). A bright young lawyer from a politically influential family (her mother-in-law was the famous Violet Alva*ji*, who had been a Union Minister and the first woman to preside over the Rajya Sabha, as Deputy Chair.) Margaret*ji* had become a Rajya Sabha MP at barely 31 years of age and in the next five years, she made her mark both in Karnataka and in Delhi where she had worked closely with Mrs Gandhi. However, in 1979, when I went to meet her, Margaret*ji* and several others had been expelled from the Indira Congress for siding with Devaraj Urs, who had fallen foul of Sanjay Gandhi.

I was unaware of these intricate backstories when I blithely set off to meet her, caught up in my starry-eyed dream of power and glamour. Margaret*ji* was heavily pregnant with her fourth child, Babu (Nivedith Alva, currently a bright young political aspirant in Karnataka). She was sweet and frank; she told me that in her condition she couldn't do much for me, and the best thing would be for me to go to the old Congress office and find out for myself if that's where I wanted to be. The Congress(S) or the old Congress was headed by Chief Minister Devaraj Urs in Karnataka.

Devaraj Urs was a towering figure in Karnataka politics. He had sided with Indira both times that she had split the party, first in 1969 when the Indian National Congress split into the Samstha (Congress-O) and Indira Congress (Congress R), and again in 1978, when she formed the Congress(I). He became the Chief Minister after winning the elections both times. But he developed differences with Indira in 1979 and joined the other Congress, the Congress (S). Locally, the Congress (S) was referred to as the Ursu Congress. Urs was able to continue as the CM, even after switching loyalties as he had the support of many MLAs (Members of Legislative Assembly). In the 1980 Lok Sabha elections, however, his party won just one out of the 28 seats in Karnataka. Enticed by R. Gundu Rao, most of Urs' MLAs deserted him to rejoin Congress(I). Urs was ousted as Chief Minister and replaced by Gundu Rao in January 1980. That was my first direct experience of 'horse-trading' which is so much part of Indian politics.

I had a ringside view of the deal that was conducted in the house of Hajee Abdul Sattar Sait, an MLC (Member of State Legislative Council) who had switched sides from Urs to Indira Gandhi before the elections. As soon as I got wind that all the MLAs had been invited for a get-together, I promptly positioned myself in Sait's house and watched wide-eyed all that transpired. C.K. Jaffer Sharief, another Congress stalwart, was against the deal-making. He wanted fresh elections to be called for the Assembly instead of a government made up of defectors. But Gundu Rao and F.M. Khan, a powerful Congress leader, prevailed and Sharief never forgave them. This led to a continued clash of these titans over the years.

However, all that was much later, and Devaraj Urs was very much the all-powerful Chief Minister when I went to the Ursu Congress office, as directed by Margaret*ji*. I found myself at a loss as no one seemed bothered to engage with me. I walked through the office and didn't like the vibes of the place. I certainly didn't see myself fitting in the organisation, so I decided to walk to the Congress(I) office, the Indira Congress. There were very few people there but there was a buzz about the place. The party workers seemed ready to welcome anybody who would campaign for it, and I was drawn to the place. I felt I had a good chance to be successful in politics if I joined this party.

Campaign Trail

I was 31 when I joined the Congress party, and I started at the bottom, as a humble party worker. I became a primary member of the party by paying Rs 10. I plunged into campaigning soon after, with the general elections being announced for the very next year, in January 1980. There was no time to relax and I worked very hard. I could communicate with voters fluently in Urdu, English, and Tamil; I didn't yet know Kannada well enough to speak it fluently, so I used to accompany another party worker, Kempamma, on campaigns. All of us used our own vehicles as the Indira Congress had no money. All the party workers were pooling in their resources and did all they could for the party.

We went to DJ Halli (Devara Jeevanahalli, a locality in north Bengaluru) and were delighted to see little children singing *Indira ko vote do, aadhi roti khayenge Indira ko layenge.* (Vote for Indira! We'll eat half a roti and bring back Indira, meaning that they would sacrifice their food to get Indira back to power.) When we went to Shivajinagar (in central Bengaluru) though, I had a shock. It is a tough neighbourhood, a rowdy *mohalla*. One of them started abusing me, '*Tu suvar hain, tere baap harami hai* (You are a pig, your father is a bastard).' I could not understand what my father had to do with it and asked him, '*Mere baap kaun hai tumko malum hai kya?* (Do you know who my father is?).' He replied angrily, '*Haina woh kutta* (he is that dog),' and mentioned the name of the local MP. I told them, '*Woh na mera chacha hai, na mera baap, mai, Congress party ke liye vote mangney ayee houn*. (He's neither my uncle nor my father, I have come to seek votes for the Congress party).'

Those years, if you wanted a passport, you had to go to an MP and get their signature on the application. Applicants hated one of the MPs in particular because he charged the locals Rs 25 to sign their requests for passports. It was a steep amount for the poor people in that area those days and they hated him. And while they waited outside his house, his wife apparently would set her dogs on them. I think that I would have been lynched that day had I not quickly clarified that I was not related to him.

I attended Indira Gandhi's election rally in 1979, as a party worker. She was campaigning across the length and breadth of the country for the 1980 general elections. She was several hours late for the rally at the Gymkhana Ground, which was filled with people; there was no place even for a matchstick as lakhs of people had come to see and hear her. They were not hired attendees, as has become the norm at political rallies these days, and in any case, she didn't have the funds. She was the darling of the masses because she had implemented many initiatives for the poor such as pensions for the aged and widows. Her slogan of *Garibi Hatao* (Banish Poverty) resonated with the downtrodden.

When she finally addressed the crowd, it was 2 a.m. and I can't describe the euphoria I witnessed; it was like being at a live sporting event. She bowled us over with her charisma. Years later, Rajiv Gandhi had a similar reception at the very same grounds when he became general secretary of the party.

It was a very difficult time for the Congress and I know that in Karnataka, owing to the paucity of funds, some of the leaders borrowed money to fund the election campaigns of the candidates. Despite this constraint, Indira swept the Congress into power with a resounding majority, and in Karnataka, the party won 27 out of 28 Lok Sabha seats. Urs resigned as CM.

Hands Off!

Prominent leaders from my community did not like my joining politics. I was a Muslim woman from a wealthy and influential family, and I dressed fashionably and looked glamorous. They said I wouldn't be able to handle the lecherous men in politics. Ironically, these same men later became lecherous too!

I began assisting Margaret*ji* in 1981 (who had by then reconciled with Indira Gandhi), and in 1982, she made me the president of the Bangalore City wing of the Mahila Congress. I had also become a member of the Indian Red Cross and president of the Minority Welfare Association, Jayamahal (in Bengaluru).

As convener of the City Mahila Congress during 1982-83, I began to work among slum dwellers in utterly neglected areas like DJ Halli, Chandra Layout, Muslim Colony, and Shivajinagar. I used to go to the Congress office every Monday to meet all the party workers and sort out issues like ration cards, telephone connections, and LPG (cooking gas) connections; all the things for which ordinary people needed recommendations from prominent people. It's also much easier to help with such things when your party is in power. Gundu Rao was the Chief Minister then. Those were the days of landlines and getting a telephone connection was very difficult, but through my party, I was able to help people.

That said, as an MLC even I had to beg to get a telephone connection! Experiences like these motivated me to work harder and aspire to someday get to a position where I could help the poorest of the poor and ease their suffering. I was delighted when years later Rajiv Gandhi ushered in the telecom revolution and Narasimha Rao did away with the dreaded Licence Raj.

I was actively involved in the 1983 Assembly elections in which Chief Minister Gundu Rao had high hopes of riding back to power. He hailed from Kodagu where he was regarded as a darling son and was confident of winning the election. He was confident that while he had the native voters in his thrall, the migrant Muslim workers from neighbouring Kerala who had settled in the district would also vote for him.

My uncle, Ebrahim Sulaiman Sait, was president of the Indian Union Muslim League (IUML) which was planning to contest three seats in Karnataka. When it approached the Congress for an electoral alliance for these seats, the Grand Old Party snubbed the request. Gundu Rao reached out to all the Muslim members in the Congress to campaign for him. At the party's request, I went to Chennai to meet my uncle and seek his support. But it was too late, the IUML's parliamentary board had decided to go it alone.

The Gokak agitation, which sought primacy for the local language, had scared the migrants who feared that they would lose their jobs if the Gokak Report was implemented. During the campaigns in Kodagu, I formed the impression that it would be a tough fight.

Although I was a greenhorn in politics, my political instincts told me that the Congress would not have it easy this time as the Muslim workers in the plantations would vote *en bloc* for the League. Campaigning with my party colleague Vijayalakshmi Ram Bhat, I met voters who bad-mouthed Gundu Rao. It confirmed my view that the Congress would lose, and I promptly took this information to the party's top brass. They pooh-poohed my fears, coming as it did from a political novice.

As luck would have it, I had the opportunity to voice my fears to Indira Gandhi. She had come to campaign for the party and was staying at the Raj Bhavan in Bengaluru. I wanted to see her off, and stood just outside her door. As she walked out, I said to her, 'Madam, we are losing the election.' It stopped her in her tracks. She turned back and asked Gundu Rao who was following her, 'Gundu, what is this girl saying?'

He brushed it off, saying that I was new to politics and didn't know what I was talking about. But I was proved right. Gundu Rao himself lost his seat along with many Congress stalwarts. This ushered in the first non-Congress government to power in Karnataka, a historic event that would forever change the shape of the state's politics. Ramakrishna Hegde of the Janata Party became the Chief Minister of a coalition government.

Meanwhile, I continued to apply myself to party work, helping the constituents in whatever way I could. My hard work began to pay dividends, despite a lukewarm response from prominent male Muslim leaders in the party. Five years after joining the Congress, I was given a ticket to contest the Bangalore City Corporation elections to become a corporator from the Shivajinagar constituency, in 1983. The Janata Party had come to power in Karnataka, and within six months, Chief Minister Hegde called for civic/local body elections in the state.

Darby Filly vs Gymkhana Horse

I was a 36-year-old political novice and was raring to make my debut. It would turn out to be the first and the last time that I contested a direct election. The seat that I was contesting for was a reserved seat for a woman, and opposing me was Mumtaz Begum, a schoolteacher, who was backed by the Janata Party. The media went to town dubbing the contest as 'Darby Filly vs Gymkhana Horse'. I plunged eagerly into the heat and dust of the campaign which soon became a political minefield.

To start with, Jaffer Sharief, the Union Minister of State for Railways in Prime Minister Indira Gandhi's cabinet and the strongest Muslim leader from Karnataka (though I have had many differences with him, I am the first to acknowledge that there never has been anyone like him, before or since, in the Muslim community in Karnataka), point-blank refused to help me.

F.M. Khan who was the general secretary of the Karnataka Youth Congress and an MLC, had become a Rajya Sabha member and treasurer of the Congress Parliamentary Party. He was very helpful and showed me the ropes. A key element is to know how to make the voters list and he helped me with that.

My husband, Hassan, was sweet and supportive. He went through all the dirty gullies full of human and animal excrement. He campaigned for me earnestly. All the other family members, including my brothers and sister, kept out. My father was furious with me as he had told me not to contest a direct election as he knew it was a dirty game.

My opponent, Mumtaz Begum, was backed by M. Raghupathy, a Minister in Hegde's cabinet, who took up the election as a prestige issue. His right-hand man was Ameen Sait, who was popularly known as 'Cinderella' Ameen. Cinderella was the name of his shop where he sold much sought-after imported goods in those days.

My opponents told voters that Nafees Fazal starts her day in a club and then goes to the Race Course and plays cards, accusing me of all sorts of things that I never did. For the Muslim voters, such behaviour was anathema; they will never tolerate a Muslim drinking or gambling or going to the races. They would say '*Nafees Fazal murdabad* (Down with Nafees Fazal)' at public meetings. They called me a *randi* (prostitute). I was a political novice, and still learning the intricacies of an election; the character assassination that I was subjected to was very hurtful.

I won the voters' confidence by pointing out that I hadn't entered politics to make money. They knew that my family owned the popular Fazals store, one of the most popular stores on Commercial Street. It was a landmark in Bangalore's posh shopping district. I told voters that I had come to help them with whatever they wanted. I sincerely thought I could do much for them in the two-year term as a corporator.

The electorate consisted of *pehelwans*, gymkhana horse owners, and butchers, and they were all happy to work for my campaign. I had opened an office in every *mohalla*, which involved a lot of funds in maintaining the premises, operational expenses, and other sundry items. I had to spend money to grow our voter list, and I had to spend quite a few thousand each week.

The campaign workers would organise roadside public meetings every evening and I would have to address crowds of random people who gathered there. Though I studied at a boarding school, for the life of me, I couldn't speak in public. My life was becoming tough but then I had chosen to take the hard road. I maintained a confident and brave front in public. At home, I used to cry about all the rumours the Opposition spread about me. I was still young and inexperienced and hadn't toughened up.

Meanwhile, the campaign was heating up. Those were days when the Middle East had begun to hire cheap labour from India. For the unemployed youth in India, the prospect of a job abroad was like a passport to riches. My adversary from the Janata Party promised lucrative jobs in the Middle East for the young men in Shivajinagar. The voters fell for the bait, hook, line, and sinker.

I was raised with a different set of values and I couldn't give any assurances or promises to my voters if I was not able to fulfil them. I soon learnt that in politics, promises are written on water. I lost by just 67 votes, which wasn't too bad. The ruling party won a landslide victory in the Bangalore City Corporation, capturing a total of 36 per cent of the votes, apart from getting control of 45 of the 166 town municipalities for which elections were held (*India Today*). And Mumtaz Begum, who defeated me, went on to become the Mayor of the BBMP (Bruhat Bengaluru Mahanagara Palike) later.

My in-laws were gleeful that I lost the elections. They perhaps hoped that the defeat meant I would bid politics goodbye. On the contrary, it just whetted my appetite. If my feisty nature hadn't been apparent until then, it was in the forefront now. I don't give up just like that. If I decide to do something, I go the whole hog.

When I went home after my defeat, my mother-in-law told me to quit politics and just stay at home to be a mother and wife. I immediately shot back, 'No way! I will not run away. I will stay and do what I have set out to do in politics, but you may please leave and take your son away too.' Luckily for me, my husband didn't take offence. My dear Hassan continued to be my rock, and his calm disposition, quiet strength and words of assurance helped settle my tense nerves at several moments.

Though I had lost, I had made my presence felt and my political stock went up. I soon realised how much the voters were beginning to acknowledge me. A little after the elections, a group of 160 men from my constituency were stranded in the national capital, New Delhi.

Unscrupulous agents had promised these men from Shivajinagar high paying jobs abroad but had cheated them, leaving them stranded at the airport where they had gone to fly on to the promised jobs.

I set to work immediately, calling all my contacts in Delhi to ensure that they were given timely help to get back home. I got the bogus Arabs and Ameen Sait, Raghupathy's right-hand man, who was involved in the racket, arrested. My intervention won me their support and admiration and it also helped me expand my circle of influence in a constituency where I hoped to contest again: I set the bar a little higher this time and hoped to get an opportunity to contest the Assembly elections. But it was not going to be an easy task, as I was soon to learn.

Jail & Bail

Every politician has to go through baptism in political fire. Mine happened quite early in my political life although the rewards would take several years to come.

In March 1984, a young man, Sayed Umar alias Munna, from Rangingalli in Shivajinagar, died in police custody. Because of the social work I had done, some affected people including his relatives approached me to help them get the body released from police custody so that they could give him a decent religious burial.

This is the summary of what had happened: three police constables picked Munna up from his home in Shivajinagar on 9 March 1984, charging him with stealing a bicycle. The police version is that while in the lock-up, Munna complained of chest pain and they rushed him to the government-run Bowring Hospital where he breathed his last. The next morning, around 5.30 a.m., the police, after moving the body to the Victoria Hospital, knocked on the doors of Munna's house and told his father, Sayed Gafar, about Munna's death at the hospital.

But even before Munna was rushed to Bowring Hospital, there were rumours that some people had heard his cries of pain from within the Shivajinagar police station. After he died, the public felt that Munna was tortured to death by the police. By 3 p.m. on 10 March 1984, hundreds of people gathered in front of the police station demanding immediate suspension of the policemen involved in the alleged torture. Soon the situation turned violent.

India's first English weekly, *The City Tab*, reported at that time that stones, soda bottles, and broken tube lights were flung at the police. There were even attempts to set the police station on fire. Fearing the worst, the policemen arranged for the burial of Munna late in the night at the JC Nagar Masjid burial grounds. This further infuriated the protestors.

The violence didn't subside even after Union Minister for Railways Jaffer Sharief, the MP from the area, addressed a peace meeting. Tempers ran high. Following repeated attacks on the police from the area's narrow by-lanes and gullies, the police picked up about a 100 people, causing further unrest and tension in the area. Some of them were arrested from their homes on charges of throwing soda water bottles and stones at the cops. While two persons were injured, 60 rounds of rubber bullets and 500 tear gas shells were burst. Sixty platoons of police were pressed into service.

Between 9 and 11 March, in two days of rioting, shops were set on fire. Almost 40 vehicles were damaged and 82 policemen were injured. Police had burst 1,084 teargas shells and opened five rounds of fire. It was like a battle zone with the people and the police facing off over the death of young Munna in police custody.

In this mayhem, I was accused of instigating violence and was arrested. This is how the events leading to my arrest unfolded.

A local leader, Jaani Pahalwan, sought my help to retrieve Munna's body from the hospital. '*Abhi Munna mar gaya, uska janaazad chahiye* (now Munna is dead, we need his body),' he told me and asked me to do something. I saw desperate hope in Jaani's eyes and unhesitatingly set off in my car. When I reached Shivajinagar, the area was wracked by tension, violence simmered in the air. The angry public didn't buy the police version of Munna's death. His father, a self-respecting man, said that his son's body was badly lacerated, swollen, and wounded.

Broadway, contrary to its name, is a narrow road in Shivajinagar where the police station is located. With people blocking the entrance, I got out of my car, and was immediately surrounded by groups of youth, who were calling me *behen* (sister).

I began walking to the station, even as cries for justice rent the air. Emotions were running high. The police too didn't want any unsavoury incidents to happen. Srinivas Alva, who was a Deputy Commissioner of Police, gave me the mike to talk. He asked me to address the crowd and appeal for peace. I agreed to speak and began with a customary prelude to a pilgrimage, *Naare Takbeer,* and back came the resounding response from the crowd, *Allah Hu Akbar*. Then everything went berserk. I watched with horror as my words were misconstrued as a call to arms!

The police started a lathi charge and tear-gassed us. I walked through the tear gas, my eyes watering and feeling faint. The boys in the area knew me because I had contested the elections. To keep me safe, they opened the gate of a *gujari* shop (such shops sell spare parts for vehicles), and downed the shutter. My car was parked near the

Elgin theatre which was a part of Shivajinagar. My driver called up Hassan and told him '*Amma ko kya ho gaya malum nahi. Idhar bahut galata chalraye* (I don't know what's happened to madam. There's a lot of trouble here).' But Hassan could not get to where I was because the whole area was burning.

Meanwhile, I seethed at the injustice done to Munna and made my way to the Victoria Hospital where his body was kept. Along the way, at Vasanth Nagar, I met A.R. Infant, who was the Deputy Commissioner of Police. He told me not to go to the hospital as I could be arrested, but I went anyway. '*Jo hota hai, hone do* (whatever happens, let it happen),' I told him. I cannot stand to see injustice. Munna was all set to go to Muscat the next day to take up a new job and begin a new life with the help of his sister who had settled there with her husband.

But the police had picked him up and beaten him. There were cuts on his body. You know what the police can do. While I was at the hospital, a police officer, named Chandrasekhar, came there and said to me, 'You are under arrest for creating a law and order problem.'

The officer was in charge of the police station next to the Minto Eye Hospital. After telling me that I was under arrest, he asked if I would go to the station in my car or in the police van. I opted to go in my car. Chandrasekhar was a very refined man, and he was kind and courteous to me. At 7 p.m. he told me that I had better get myself released, since I knew Police Commissioner P.G. Halarnkar and Director General of Police B.N. Garudachar.

I rang up the Commissioner, and while he obviously knew what was happening, he didn't help me. The police asked for an undertaking that I would not visit the Shivajinagar area again but weren't satisfied with it. I was not let off. They put me in a police van just like in a Hindi movie, and I did not know where they were taking me. There were no cell phones those days, but my driver had been able to alert my husband. Hassan rushed to the station along with his friend Riyaz. They landed there in time, just as the van was pulling away. Riyaz bodily obstructed the van, while Hassan jumped into the van and accompanied me to a Remand Home for Women.

The Police Commissioner backed the Shivajinagar police. The Commissioner justified the strong-arm tactics to put down alleged rowdyism in the area. He claimed that the lathi charges and tear gas firing in fact showed that the police had exercised tremendous restraint. The facts on the ground reflected otherwise. Police were barging into homes in the area and raining blows left and right, alienating the locals against them.

Caught in the cross hairs, we felt that the ruling Janata Party was out to harass Congress workers like us. Apart from me, a case was also filed against others, including Ibrahim, for making inflammatory speeches. I learnt later that Chief Minister Hegde had authorized the police to quell the violence in Shivajinagar with an iron hand.

In my journey in politics, I also learnt that sometimes you can be right and yet become wrong, simply by being in the wrong place at the wrong time. Looking back, I feel that I should have stopped to think before heading off like Joan of Arc. At that moment, I was swept away by political naiveté and my eagerness to help people. For the first time in my life, I understood not only the enormous power of the police but also the helplessness of a public leader who is often caught between the devil and the deep blue sea.

I felt the local police inspector could have been more proactive in stemming the unrest at the beginning itself. There were complaints from the people about this particular sub inspector, but his bosses seemed to fully back whatever he did in the name of law and order.

Even as the tension showed signs of ebbing, fresh trouble broke out in another part of the city on 12 March 1984, over an unrelated matter. An English weekly called *Voice of Karnataka* published news that V. Srinivasan, the Janata Party MLA from Yelahanka who was also the chairman of the Karnataka Food and Civil Supplies Corporation, was targeting fair price shops owned by Muslims (*India Today*, 15 April, 1984). This news stoked the anger of Muslims who were already enraged over Munna's death. Mobs were baying for Srinivasan's blood and crowds blocked roads in the Bamboo Bazaar area near Shivajinagar.

Tannery Road and Moore Road were burning with large-scale arson and looting. The police clamped a dawn-to-dusk curfew and when that didn't quell the riots, they resorted to firing which resulted in seven people being killed. The magazine's editors were also arrested for inciting communal hatred. It also became a political blame game with the ruling party accusing the Congress and vice versa.

Behind Bars

Meanwhile, I was shattered by my arrest. I had hitherto led a sheltered and pampered existence. I hadn't experienced anything as drastic as what had happened to me. I knew my family would be greatly embarrassed at my arrest, and it made me doubt myself and my decision to enter politics.

To be fair, the police did not ill-treat me. After my arrest, I was sent to the remand home where I was lodged in the company of bar dancers. These women were very kind; despite their own problems, they seemed to walk with a swing to their hips and were good-humoured. When they saw me disconsolate and exhausted, they consoled me. 'Cheer up, Madam, arrests are a routine thing for us; it happens all the time. In one or two nights, they will let you go,' they reassured me.

I thanked my stars for having had the good sense to learn to speak a bit of Kannada for I could speak with them and while away some time at least. In the midst of my shame and despair, the irony of the situation didn't escape me – my father had forbidden me from learning Bharatanatyam as it was considered a courtesan's dance and now, I was stuck in the company of girls who danced in bars! My father wept buckets when he heard of my arrest.

Political prisoners are high-risk and watched carefully as they might die by suicide and land the officials and government in trouble. When my brother Ameen and brother-in-law Muneer brought me fruit and biscuits, the warden made them taste the food in front of her before giving it to me. The staff at the remand home had a huge headache from my hysterics. I wept and threatened to swallow the diamond on my finger ring. The nerve-wracking experience of Munna's death, the riot and my arrest had flipped my mind. And coming from a privileged background, I found it very difficult to spend two days in the remand home.

What shamed me even more was that my name was listed alongside infamous and notorious elements. One of them was Koli Fayaz who used to sell poultry before becoming one of the leading gangsters in Bangalore. And I had to appear in court each week and stand along with such criminals.

In any case, I decided to fight the case filed against me, and clear my name. The legal fight took several years but I was determined to absolve myself without falling at any *neta*'s feet for help. I had too much self-respect and honour to safeguard. Besides, my passport was impounded for five years and I could not travel abroad without the court's permission.

The ignominy of having my name on the police records was painful for a convent-educated woman like me who had never stepped into a police station or even a remand home for that matter. Dealing with the police, going to the courts, and talking and giving briefs to the lawyers from time to time was taking its toll on me. Family members began to advise me to keep away from politics; the police case wasn't good for my reputation and besides, I had two young daughters to worry about.

I knew they meant well and had my welfare at heart, but I could not walk away from public life. I had set my sights on a life in politics, and I realised that it had me in its thrall. There was no looking back now, and I had to follow my destiny despite the hard path. Back then I never imagined that I would end up becoming the first Muslim woman minister in the South of India. I never imagined that my life would be a role model for aspiring young girls from my community.

There were many dark clouds in my life in the early years. Despite the twists and turns in my life, I persevered, and I hope it smoothed the path for my worthy successors from the community and for all women.

The exact cause of the death of 25-year-old Munna remains a mystery to me even to this day, unless of course I go with the police version of the day. What I went through in trying to get justice for Munna gave me strength in my journey in political life which sustained me several years later. More importantly, as I realised later, it brought me to the attention of my idol.

After I was arrested in March 1984, one day I got a call from R.K. Dhawan, Indira Gandhi's personal secretary and confidant. He said, 'Madam wants to meet you.' My arrest in the Munna incident had become national news and it had come to the notice of Mrs Gandhi. I went to Delhi to meet her. 'Well done,' she said, patting me on my shoulder. Then she called for Jaffer Sharief and my uncle Ebrahim Sulaiman Sait and told them that Muslims had to join the mainstream, and women like me had to be encouraged in politics. Those were her exact words. My uncle told me later, 'Indira*ji* has a lot of regard for you and has told us we should bring in more progressive Muslim women into the mainstream.'

Sharief's Astrologer

Jaffer was insecure though and probably feared that if Indira*ji* said that I had potential, then I could become a threat to his power hold at some time. Soon after, he asked to meet me. He said, 'I am taking you somewhere and you have to promise me that you will follow the advice you hear. If you hear that politics is not for you, you must go and look after your shop and stay away from politics.'

I was willing to take the risk and agreed. We went in Jaffer's car to meet an astrologer called Chandrasekhar Swamy, in Vijayanagar. Jaffer told Swamy that I was going through a bad patch and asked him to check if I had a political future. Although Chandrasekhar Swamy did not have my *janam kundli* (birth chart), he read my palm and started laughing. When Jaffer questioned him, probably hoping that he would say that he saw a big zero in politics, Swamy said,

'She has the *raja yoga* and will become a minister.' While Jaffer was dumbstruck, I was delighted; I knew my destiny was calling!

Building a Profile

The years that followed were a very difficult period for me. A ray of sunshine in the dismal time was that I was appointed as a judge in the Consumer Disputes Redressal Forum, thanks to Margaret*ji*'s good offices. Margaret*ji* continued to support me throughout those low days.

I was the first woman judge of the forum; I have this to my credit. It is a very powerful forum, and a judge has the rights of a superintendent of police. It was also long hours of work, and I would be tired.

This was the time I also began to hone my public speaking skills. I also took F.M. Khan's advice to learn Kannada seriously and engaged a tutor. He told me, 'If you don't learn Kannada, go back and sit in your shop (Fazal's) and design your clothes.' While I very much liked to design and wear nice clothes, my ambitions lay in politics, and I was determined to do everything by the book to achieve it.

For good measure, I also engaged an Urdu teacher as I realised that with my convent education and as a native Tamilian, my Urdu was far from perfect. If I had to communicate with the constituents of my adopted homeland, I would have to master both Kannada and Urdu. It was not easy, and I slogged, but I learnt both languages very well.

Today, I would say I speak better Kannada than Tamil; speaking the local language comes instinctively to me and I feel happy that I made the effort to integrate wholeheartedly. I strongly believe that people who move to a new place should learn the language of their new homeland. I feel it is very important to know the language especially when you need to interact with people.

Mahila Convention

The All-India Mahila Convention was held in Bangalore in September 1984, at the Palace grounds. Margaret*ji* was the National Convenor of the All-India Mahila Congress and was entrusted with the task of organising it. Thirty thousand delegates came from all across India, and I was completely involved in playing host to them, as part of the local organising team.

Mrs Indira Gandhi presided over the convention; Margaret*ji*, who had appointed me president of the women's wing for Bangalore City, gave me the honour of garlanding Indira*ji*. Standing a few feet behind her was her bodyguard, Beant Singh, who would go on to assassinate the Prime Minister just a month later.

I continued to work hard for the party and the people as the Convenor of the Bangalore City Mahila Congress, and began to help out with the *loan melas* introduced by Janardhan Poojary. He was the Union Minister of State for Finance, and those days there was a lot of *dhamaka* (noise) about loan *melas*. Poojary was a workaholic and I too worked very hard to help people, staying up through the night until early morning. Poojary's base was the Kumara Krupa Guest House. People would come in droves, and we had to guide them in filling out their applications for loans.

The loans were part of a self-empowerment scheme. Each applicant was given a loan of up to Rs 20,000 to help them become self-employed; it was big money in those days. They used it to buy push carts; we also used to distribute sewing machines. But I am sad to say that Poojary never knew how some unworthy people availed of the financial help but didn't use it for the purpose it was meant for.

A Wake-up Call

In 1989, Rajiv Gandhi was the Prime Minister, and I was in Delhi lobbying for a ticket for the upcoming Assembly elections. I got a call at 2 a.m. on my landline; Naseer Ahmed, an up-and-coming politician from Karnataka who's currently an MLC, was on the line and said, '*Bhabhi,* MOS wants to talk to you.' Jaffer Sharief was then the Minister of State for Railways and when I met him, he told me that he wanted me to be the candidate from Shivajinagar for the Assembly elections. Those years MPs were very important people and could choose their own candidates. He showed a slip of paper which had the names of the candidates he had recommended for various seats. He told me, 'I promise you that I will get you the seat, we want a new face.' I was delighted and thanked him profusely.

But my joy didn't last long, as Jaffer proved to be duplicitous. The list that he sent had a different set of names and mine was missing from it. It wasn't hard to find this out as there are always leaks in the Prime Minister's Office. After promising me the seat, Jaffer had instead recommended K. Rahman Khan's name (who later became the Union Minister of Minority Affairs and Deputy Chairman of the Rajya Sabha. But Rahman wanted Binnypet constituency, so the ticket went to A.K. Anantha Krishna). There was nothing left for me to do in Delhi and so I decided to pack my bags and leave for Bengaluru.

An MP in My Loo!

I always stayed at The Claridges in Delhi, and I was fuming in my room when F.M. Khan came over to commiserate with me. I complained bitterly that whatever chances I had of getting a ticket were gone. To mollify me, he ordered my favourite Chinese cuisine for lunch and while we waited for it, out of the blue, the front desk called to say that Jaffer was on his way to my room.

I was stunned at first and then began to panic. F.M. Khan and Jaffer were adversaries; Jaffer was one of the people responsible for F.M. Khan's expulsion from the Congress. What would happen when Jaffer, the all-powerful MP, walked into my room and saw me with a disgraced MP! I didn't want to risk whatever slim chance that might have remained of getting the ticket.

F.M. Khan didn't seem too worried; his only concern seemed to be about food, 'What will this *buddha* (old man) eat?' he asked me when I told him Jaffer was heading to my room. I pushed F.M. Khan into the bathroom and locked it. I admonished him to stay quiet until I opened it.

Jaffer had come to act out another pretence that he was not responsible for my name missing on the list of those recommended for the Assembly ticket. I couldn't pay much attention as I was anxious that he might ask to use the toilet. He was highly diabetic and had to use the washroom frequently. I was sweating buckets throughout!

In the elections, Anantha Krishna won against Roshan Baig, who was then with the Janata Dal. As a disciplined party worker, I worked for the party's chosen candidate, and was the election agent for Anantha Krishna. Roshan Baig lost by 89 votes, and his goons surrounded me shouting, 'Nafees Fazal *murdabad* (Down with Nafees Fazal)'. They alleged that I had carried away a ballot box, and they also filed a case against me and the party.

The Stars Align

I was sorely disappointed at not getting the Assembly ticket but didn't give up hope. I always tried, I always fought, even when the odds were against me. I was determined that I would not let the local Muslim men pull me down. I used to go to Delhi every two years and lobby for an MLC seat. In 1994, Margaret*ji* promised to help me.

Over the years, she had tested my loyalty; I had to prove myself repeatedly because I was also associated with F.M. Khan. He was part of Sanjay Gandhi's 'stormtroopers' as Margaret*ji* called them and she was wary of me because he was my supporter. F.M. Khan had also been thrown out of the party for defying the party high command. But I proved to Margaret*ji* that I was not under his influence. She had begun to trust me and put my name up for nomination to the Legislative Council. Once again, Jaffer tried to block it. He went to Margaret*ji* and S.M. Krishna and asked them to nominate his son. But both of them refused Jaffer's request.

Margaret*ji* was a Union Minister, and I accompanied her to Arjun Singh's house for an *iftar* party. P.V. Narasimha Rao, who was the Prime Minister, was also present. I was introduced to him and spent some time exchanging civilities. Tariq Anwar, who was also there, came up to me to say, '*Aap ko ticket mil gaya samjho. Buddha kisi ke saath baat nahi karte, aap ke saath joke kiya*' (You can be assured of getting your ticket. The old man doesn't talk to anyone but has even exchanged jokes with you).'

One swallow does not a summer make, so it took the collective efforts of many well-wishers for my dream to be realised. Dhawan also spoke up for me, saying that I was a proven leader and had gone to jail for helping people, and not for smuggling or such crimes. Then Salman Khurshid also helped me. He was the External Affairs Minister. He wrote to Narasimha Rao stating that we don't get women like me in politics. 'She is progressive, and I think our community needs her.' The fact that I am a progressive Muslim woman played an important part. SMK, who was the Deputy Chief Minister of Karnataka (a post he accepted reluctantly at Margaret*ji*'s persuasion), also wrote a letter recommending my nomination. But in the end, it was Margaret*ji* who saw me through. She called me to the Central Hall of Parliament and introduced me to Kalyani Shankar, a journalist, who was very close to Narasimha Rao. Kalyani took a liking to me and invited me over for a chat where she quizzed me with political questions.

It was 11 at night and I was at home in Bengaluru when the phone rang. I heard SMK's voice, saying, *Insha Allah.* He was in the Karnataka Bhavan in Delhi and called me as soon as the names of the candidates were cleared by the party high command. By God's grace, I got the party's nomination. I got it in the Muslim quota; I was the only woman, and I was a Muslim.

There was so much *hungama,* a lot of ruckus, the next day. Phone calls kept coming from people congratulating me. There are highs and lows in life, and this was one of the best days of my life.

There were some panicky moments when the time came to file my papers and it would have been a near miss. My name had been misspelled and the returning officer pointed it out and said he couldn't accept it. Even before I got this information, other hopeful candidates ran to Veerappa Moily (who was the Chief Minister then) and said that their papers were in order, and they ought to be chosen.

To his credit, Moily stood firm and said that I was the choice of the High Command. Jabir, a coffee planter who is a family friend, ran to the City Corporation office and got the error rectified in a couple of hours. My papers were in order by 2 p.m. and Moily did see me through. He gave me a choice of voters too from among the MLAs, but I left it to him to decide. I was the only woman in the fray, there were 10 men.

I was elected as an MLC for the first term in 1994. I became an MLC in July; in the Assembly polls in December, the Congress lost. The Janata Dal came to power and H.D. Deve Gowda became the Chief Minister. I sat in the Opposition benches. The best way to become a good legislator is to sit in the Opposition and participate in the question time and put up supplementary questions. This knowledge was of great use to me when I became a minister later; I could anticipate the questions that would be asked and I was always prepared.

As a first-time MLC, I had no training and didn't know how to pose supplementary questions in the House. It was M.C. Nanaiah of the Janata Dal, and Dr M.R. Tanga and D.H. Shankaramurthy of the BJP, who trained me. Being a fast learner, I quickly picked up the ropes. I did not want to be a Council member; I wanted to be elected by the masses. But though I was denied that opportunity, I did my best and participated actively. My questions used to be reported quite often in leading newspapers.

Rewarded at Last

Efforts were underway for S.M. Krishna to become the president of the KPCC (Karnataka Pradesh Congress Committee), in the run-up to the 1999 Assembly elections. R.T. Narayan was a close friend of S.M. Krishna and gathered legislators in his room at the West End; he asked everyone to lobby for S.M. Krishna to replace Dharam Singh. Polls were in October, and it was quite tough to change with seven months to go. D.K. Shivakumar and I lobbied for S.M. Krishna who promised me that if he became KPCC president, he would take care of my political interests.

It was a marathon effort, as Sonia Gandhi referred to SMK as a 'white collared' politician who couldn't woo voters in the rural areas. DK and I conducted a round of lunch and dinner diplomacy with SMK's adversaries in the party. To name a few, R.L. Jalappa, Chandrasekhar Murthy and Jaffer Sharief didn't have anything against SMK personally but felt that changing the party president with just seven months left for the elections was cutting it too fine.

The elections to the Karnataka Assembly were held simultaneously with the General Elections in 1999. The Congress won the Assembly elections with a thumping majority, securing 132 of the 224 seats. The National Democratic Alliance comprising the BJP and the Janata Dal (United) won only 63 seats, and the Janata Dal (Secular), fronted by former Prime Minister Deve Gowda, managed to get only 10 seats.

SMK had steered the party to a handsome victory, garnering over 40 percent of the votes in the Assembly. The Congress also won 18 of the 28 Lok Sabha seats, even when the NDA returned to power at the Centre with Atal Bihari Vajpayee as Prime Minister.

As a just reward for his efforts in Karnataka, the party high command announced that SMK was its choice to be the Chief Minister. He is not one to forget a promise and my name was on his list of ministers. Not that it was easy-going, as there were too many contenders for a spot in the ministry. S.M. Krishna's wife, Prema, had become a dear friend and she played a significant role in the backroom manoeuvres. She remembers gleefully that when Ghulam Nabi Azad, the AICC (All India Congress Committee) honcho, went to their house to deliberate with S.M. Krishna, she (Prema) pulled him into the kitchen and insisted that I had to be made a Minister.

I didn't know this at the time and believed R.T. Narayan who sadistically told me that I was not going to be included amongst the ministers. I sat and cried the whole day. Everybody at home had enough of my tears.

I had just finished *maghrib* (twilight prayers), when the phone by my bedside rang. It was Ramanujam, an Intelligence officer; he said, 'Congratulations, Madam.' I asked him why he was congratulating me and he said, 'You are going to be sworn in at 3 o'clock tomorrow in Vidhana Soudha.' I can't begin to describe my joy. I prostrated myself again in gratitude before calling Hassan and my daughters.

My younger daughter, Nooraine, was working for Reuters in Hong Kong. I couldn't get her on the phone, and so I left a message: 'My tears of sorrow have turned to tears of joy. I am being sworn in tomorrow.' Meanwhile, Nooraine had already boarded a flight to Bengaluru via Mumbai, as she wanted to take me back to Hong Kong with her, to distract me from my disappointment. She didn't tell me she was coming despite hearing my message after landing in Mumbai. When she came home at 6.30 a.m. in the morning, the house erupted in celebrations. Nooraine threw her arms around me and said, 'Mama, you have made it.' All my friends and well-wishers started calling and turning up to wish me.

The day I was sworn in as a Minister, 17 October 1999, is indelibly etched in my memory. A dream that was born when I was all of 13 years old, became a reality after 20 years in politics. I was 52 years old and brimmed with both gratitude and confidence. I wore a simple *Kanjeevaram* sari, cream with mustard, which was gifted to me by Prema. The ceremony was on the steps of the Vidhana Soudha, and thousands of people were crowding all the way to the High Court, on the opposite side. As I stood facing them and took the oath of office, I beamed with happiness and expressed heartfelt gratitude to the destiny that had led to the culmination of my dream.

In an important win for women, the new council of ministers demonstrated that it valued women. Discarding the usual practice of including just one woman as a token representative, S.M. Krishna was the first, and so far, the only Chief Minister who offered berths to four women in his council of ministers. Rani Satish, Motamma, Suma Vasanth and I quickly showed that we were hard workers and had rightfully earned our posts. And if we added glamour to the Vidhana Soudha, that was a bonus, with the dapper Chief Minister setting the style statement.

3

How I Became a Minister

MY EXPERIENCE OF life in politics is that of pleading. When you become a politician, you must begin pleading and then you keep on pleading. This was contrary to my nature, as I am a fighter rather than a beseecher. But I was ambitious to succeed in politics and I had to tame my ego several times. That is the price that I paid to get what I wanted.

Getting into the council of ministers of Karnataka in S.M. Krishna's cabinet as a minister of state was a hard-won victory for me. There were many detractors in the party who had tried to stop it by saying that an MLC (Member of the Legislative Council) can't be appointed a minister.

It took a lot of begging to get there, and all the begging that I did was not for my personal or direct benefit.

First, we had to lobby for S.M. Krishna to be made Karnataka PCC (Pradesh Congress Committee) president. The rationale was that if he led the party to victory in the 1999 Legislative Assembly elections, he would become the Chief Minister. The Congress won a huge majority of 132 seats and S.M. Krishna became the CM. And then all of us who had worked for him had to seek positions for ourselves. After I was chosen as a minister, there was the matter of the portfolio that was to be allotted to me: would it be Prisons or Kannada and Culture? I was considered for these departments before being allotted Medical Education, with the intervention of Prema *Akka* (S.M. Krishna's wife whom I address as my older sister) and V.G. Siddhartha (S.M. Krishna's son-in-law).

Another truth hit me in the face soon: once you get the chair, you have to do your darndest to hold on to it. This meant that you had to be on the lookout constantly for the daggers and knives that many seen and unseen enemies would be holding. How much time do you actually have to do any official work!

When I began the job, I remembered Prime Minister Narasimha Rao's advice to me when I went to thank him after I became an MLC. I met him in his office, and he said '*Jaldi kijiye mujhe jaana hai. Homework karna hai.* (Hurry up, I have to go and do my homework).' I was taken aback and asked him, '*Aap Andhra ke mukhya mantri the, ab Wazir-e-Azam hain. Aap ko homework kya zaroori hai*? (You have been the CM of Andhra and you are the PM now; why do you need to do homework?).' He said to me, '*Panchayati Raj ke baare mein baat karna hai, iske bare mein padna hai hame* (I have to speak about Panchayati Raj and I have to prepare for it).' He advised me to always go prepared for meetings and I made it a point to be meticulously prepared about my portfolio.

Having got the post, I got to work enthusiastically. The first thing that I did was to go to Dr K.G. Das, a reputed doctor and friend, and ask him, 'What am I supposed to do as medical education minister?' He told me to visit all the government hospitals and see their status. It would give me an idea of what I needed to do. So the very next day, Nooraine and I went to Victoria Hospital and found that the superintendent was missing. The scenes we saw were horrifying: A young woman with 90 per cent burns left to die on the hospital floor because no one cared to provide her any medical relief or even a human touch. Another young woman was chained to the hospital bed screaming for help – she had consumed poison in a failed suicide attempt. These women and many others like them were victims of the greed of cruel husbands and in-laws. 'Stove burst' was a convenient alibi for the ruthless murder of wives who were disposed off when they or their families couldn't keep up the supply of money to the husband and in-laws.

The victims who apparently sustained their grievous burns due to kerosene stoves bursting would be brought to the government hospitals that were in no position to care for them. On my first visit to the Victoria Hospital, I found that the ICU was locked; when the staff opened it at my request, it was bare of any equipment – there was nothing there, no oxygen or ventilator.

The suffering of the young women left a deep impression on me and my daughter. My exposure to abusive men had motivated me to help women who could not defend themselves. It became my life's mission to assist them to the best of my capacity.

I was able to pilot the move to accept the dying declaration of these women as evidence against their husbands and in-laws.

I began making surprise visits to hospitals; nobody knew who I was, in some places they thought I was the doctor. In the six months that I had been a minister, I was seen as a rising star. The media reported frequently about my work and hospital visits and interaction with patients. I didn't use my official state car and went incognito. A senior member, M.C. Nanaiah, suggested in a lighter vein in the council that I should be made 'minister for medical education and surprise inspections'!

Journalist M.D. Riti wrote on *Rediff*:

> Health Minister Nafees Fazal, a first-time minister who is known to be close to both Krishna and the Delhi high command, went undercover during her first week in office. She disguised herself as a social worker and spent a couple of hours in the burns ward of Victoria Hospital where women who suffer fire accidents or dowry-related violence are admitted. Not unexpectedly, she found callous nurses, truant doctors and unused equipment.

The Times of India reported under the headline, '**Nafees visits four hospitals**':

> The Minister of State for Medical Education, Mrs Nafees Fazal, today paid a surprise visit to four government teaching hospitals in the City and instructed the hospital superintendents to provide clean drinking water to patients, maintain the toilets properly and construct one more floor for Bowring and Lady Curzon Hospital.
>
> The Minister told the officials to install complaint boxes, and post staff to look into the grievances of patients. She took exception to the improper maintenance of the toilets. She had written to the Chief General Manager of Bangalore Telecom, Mr Padmanabhan, seeking the installation of hotlines for receiving complaints. At Victoria Hospital, she castigated the authorities for their failure in disposing of decomposed bodies at the mortuary.

My mantra has been 'A stitch in time prevents nine' and I looked for proactive measures to prevent crises. I realised that most often, I just had to lend a receptive ear to people's grievances, whether genuine or perceived. Most human problems are resolved by simply communicating with your heart.

Another headline said, '**Nafees steps in, doctors end stir**'. This was a case where around 80 postgraduate medical students from the Vani Vilas Hospital and the Victoria Hospital went on strike. A retired policeman's wife had delivered a stillborn baby but he accused the doctors of killing his baby and reportedly assaulted a duty doctor, accusing him of killing his son. I visited the labour ward with the superintendent and doctors and calmed down the agitated medicos.

I had to deal with three strikes during my tenure, one by house surgeons and another by medical internship students who wanted their stipend to be doubled. I thought their request was fair; if we expected the young doctors to see a future in the profession, they deserved to get adequate compensation. I was able to convince the Chief Minister to enhance the budget to increase the stipends and was able to defuse the students' strike. I was like a mother to them and became popular. The stand-off between the staff and management of the Sri Jayadeva Institute of Cardiology was a big problem. The staff wanted the director to be sacked and the revised pay scale to be extended to the staff, and not just doctors. I was able to persuade the staff to resume work by sending the director on leave and promising to examine their demand for revised pay scales. I was decisive and quick to respond and while the public and media appreciated it, the Opposition could only find fault with my work. Lokshakti Party state president Dr Jeevaraj Alva criticised me for responding to the striking staff, but my priority was to get them back to work.

The most thrilling occasion of my stint as Medical Education Minister was the phone-in programme on *Udaya TV*, when a caller compared me to Mother Teresa for the care I gave to needy patients. It was one of the most satisfying moments of my life.

The Price for Seeking Accountability

My portfolio Medical Education was attached to the Health and Family Welfare Ministry. One day in March 2000, a controversy erupted over a harmless remark. The media used to do the rounds in Vidhana Soudha, dropping by to see ministers who were free to interact with them. During one such impromptu meeting, one of them asked me about the unpaid dues of private hospitals that used the clinical facilities of the government teaching hospitals. I replied that these hospitals were under the purview of the health department and there was nothing I could do about it. I said that there was an overlap of functions between my department and the Health & Family Welfare department to which Medical Education was attached.

The next day's headlines set the cat amongst the pigeons! Promptly the newspapers reported that the Medical Education Minister wanted a free hand and that the two departments should be bifurcated.

'Give me a free hand: Nafees Fazal' thundered this headline and went on to add: 'Minister wants to come out of Malaka Reddy's control'. It said that 'irked by purported overlapping of functions with her senior colleagues Karnataka Health and Family Welfare Minister A.B. Malaka Reddy, Medical Education Minister Nafees Fazal has urged Chief Minister SM Krishna for bifurcation of both departments. Fazal has decided to take up the issue with the CM during the review of the medical education health and family welfare department on July 31.' To be fair, the report explained my position: 'It is not an ego problem but bifurcation is necessary in the interest of both departments'.

Health Minister Malaka Reddy was furious with me and complained to the Chief Minister who thought I was over-reaching and undermining his authority by such a public bid for more power. The CM too was furious with me. I was due for re-nomination as an MLC and this incident could not only claim my berth as a minister but also my seat in the Legislative Council. The only way I could survive the controversy was by issuing a public apology.

The issue became media fodder for quite a number of days and was pegged as 'Nafees Drama'. Sample these reports:

CM to pull up minister for her remarks

Chief Minister SM Krishna will seek a written explanation from Medical Education Minister Nafees Fazal, who has publicly asked for a bifurcation of her ministry from the Health and Family Welfare Department. Sources close to Krishna told *The Times of India* here on Thursday that he discussed the issue with some senior ministers including Health and Family Welfare Minister A B Malaka Reddy. The CM expressed his displeasure and took exception to the fact that Fazal chose to air her views through the media. Krishna expressed the view on Thursday that allocation of portfolio and work was the CM's prerogative.

Nafees says sorry for hurting Krishna

Medical Education Minister Nafees Fazal tendered an apology to Chief Minister S.M. Krishna and her other ministerial colleagues on Friday. In a statement issued here on Friday Mrs Fazal said, "At no stage did I intend to embarrass the government or mar its image. I humbly apologize for the hurt and anxiety caused to Mr Krishna and other colleagues". Mrs Fazal's apology comes in the wake of reports that Mr Krishna had taken exception to the statements made by Mrs Fazal at a press conference on Wednesday, suggesting the bifurcation of the Health and Family Welfare Department.

Mrs Fazal in her two-page apology, copies of which were released to the press, narrated what transpired between reporters and her on July 26th. "I did not call any press meet. The reporters happened to drop into my chamber at 12:30 pm on their regular rounds of the secretariat. One journalist asked why I was not able to recover lakhs of rupees owned by some of the private medical colleges to the government for using clinical facilities in state hospitals. I replied these hospitals were attached to the health department and not to the medical education department and so I could not initiate any action.

The Chief Minister who was upset over her statement reportedly issued a show-cause notice to her on Thursday seeking clarification for making a statement on the reallocation of work in the health and family welfare department. There was some confusion and loopholes in the working of the health and medical education departments which needed to be rectified. "My only intention is to give good and clean administration so that both the departments (health and medical education) would benefit and ensure speedy redressal of the problems of the people," she added.

This is the price I had to pay for seeking accountability. I wanted to be efficient and I ended up treading on powerful toes! The price for naiveté in politics can be quite high.

In an unexpected turn of events, a few months later, I was given independent charge of medical education without me asking for it! Life is strange indeed.

Many of my colleagues were jealous about my rising profile, but I went about doing my job with the same zeal. The next controversy that gave them an opportunity to come after me was the seat matrix for medical education. Private colleges had to allot certain seats for the government quota. Father Muller Medical College, a premier college in Mangaluru, unfortunately complained to a senior Congress leader from the region stating that I had 'interfered in the seat matrix'.

Yes, I did ask them to give an extra seat to the government quota, but I had done so at the behest of the Congress Working Committee members in Delhi. The working committee members wanted seats. Ghulam Nabi Azad wanted seats for Kashmiri students, someone else wanted MBBS seats, someone asked for postgraduate seats. Nobody did it for money; they just wanted to help poor and deserving students. My rivals took this issue up to Sonia Gandhi and complained about me. The management of Father Muller's was close to Oscar Fernandes, the Congress MP from Udupi and a close confidant of the Gandhi's.

The Opposition also targeted me, with the BJP claiming that I had taken money in exchange for approving three medical colleges, and that these funds were for the Congress party's use to fight the Kerala elections. As a minister, you are damned if you do and damned if you don't!

The media continued to make merry at my expense. If one day I was a heroine, another day I was a missing person, according to reports. Under the eye-catching headline **'Catch her if you can'**, the *Indian Express* claimed that 'One of the greatest challenges in a reporter's life is to contact Minister for Medical Education Nafees Fazal.' This was a day when I had rushed to be with my ailing mother and forgotten my mobile at home in my haste. Are ministers not human? However, I had learnt that if you are in public life, you need to accept some shots below the belt, however unjustified they may be.

Bribe Offers

I can say with conviction that I never took a bribe for anything, though it was offered many times. One such incident involved the trustee of a very reputed college. His son wanted to push a deal through for the purchase of medical equipment for government hospitals from a foreign company. I had a very astute and honest IAS officer as my Principal Secretary named A.K.M. Naik who felt the deal looked fraudulent. When I rejected the proposal, they offered me a hefty bribe. I refused to budge as I had no intention of allowing a foreign company to dump their condemned machinery in India.

The people behind the deal were upset with me and tried to get back at me. The college trustee spoke to the Chief Minister's close friend and confidant R.T. Narayan who, in turn, informed SMK that I had asked for a bribe of Rs 30 lakh. SMK called me up and asked me, 'Did you ask for Rs 30 lakh?' I told him, 'My maths is not that bad. When he was offering Rs 3 crore, why would I want to take Rs 30 lakh?' SMK was quite astounded. Even today I have not forgotten the name of another IAS officer who was the go-between with the foreign company, which was to supply all the medical equipment, and the trustee's son. Apart from this one incident, all the other IAS and KAS officers I had the privilege of working with were very honest and upright. To date I still consult my Private Secretary Mirza Akbarulla.

I could have happily taken the money, after all who doesn't need Rs 3 crore? I did not want the illegal money, and I did not want a bad name. Ministers and politicians often receive such bribes and perhaps take it, if not for themselves, then in order to fill the party coffers. How else would they hold on to their posts? This is how many of them operate. Nowadays the amounts offered would be several hundred crores.

At one point, B.S. Yediyurappa of the BJP tried to link my name to the Telgi counterfeit stamp paper scam. The prime accused in perhaps the biggest counterfeit case in India, Abdul Karim Ladsab Telgi ran a multi-crore counterfeit stamp paper racket, selling them in bulk to banks, stock brokerage firms and insurance companies. He is supposed to have operated in at least 18 states through 350 agents in 70 cities for 10 years before he was arrested in 2001. Obviously, such an operation could not have thrived without the connivance of officials and politicians. But Yediyurappa was completely out of bounds in hinting that I was involved. He claimed a minister's husband had connections with Telgi. I swiftly refuted the allegations as there wasn't an iota of truth in it. I went on TV and lambasted the Opposition and challenged them to prove their charges if they were true. One must act fast and hard to save one's reputation.

To complete Telgi's story, in 2007, he was convicted of the scam and sentenced to 30 years imprisonment and fined Rs 202 crore. Telgi was lodged in the Parappana Agrahara jail in Bengaluru, and when his health deteriorated he was taken to the Victoria Hospital where he died of multi-organ failure in 2017. The case made me think that perhaps the system in India encourages crooks by creating opportunities for them. Doesn't it stand to reason that if stamps and stamp papers are necessary to carry out various legal paperwork, then it's the government's job to make sure that they are available to those who need them? It's precisely because they were not available that Telgi found an opportunity and exploited it.

Chithi Aayee Hai

Another nail was hammered into my coffin because of a private party that I attended. It was hosted by Dinesh Gundu Rao, Congress MLA and son of the former Chief Minister Gundu Rao, at a popular hotel. All the senior leaders of the party were there, many of them in a private section as they didn't want to be seen drinking. The Congress party shuns it. Chief Minister S.M. Krishna was also there for some time. The next day R.T. Narayan complained to him that I had been drinking and dancing at the party. This untrue allegation deeply disappointed me and made me realise what power can do to people. For a long time I had considered him as one of my closest friends. Narayan was trying to get me axed because he thought I was getting too popular. It was a blatant lie and all of them knew that as per the diktat of the Congress party I never drink alcohol in public. I sip a glass of wine occasionally in the privacy of a friend's home, but that's the extent of my consumption. I do not enjoy drinking alcohol. As for dancing, it depends on what you consider as dancing I suppose! I recall standing with my friends and tapping my feet, and occasionally shrugging my shoulders to the beat of a song—my favourite—ironically called, 'I will survive' by Gloria Gaynor.

The double standards for women and men once again came to the fore! No one in power thought to question my male colleagues on their actions and what they did at the party. The spotlight was purely on me and my alleged misdeeds. Unaware of the tales being spun about my so-called behaviour, I was getting ready to go to The Atria hotel to attend a wedding of a family member of the chief minister. I was surprised when the CM's OSD (Officer on Special Duty) Sridhar came home and handed me a letter, 'Boss has sent this for you.' I got the shock of my life when I read it. The CM had written that my behaviour was not befitting of a minister, and that he wanted me to resign with immediate effect! It was a bolt from the blue and I could barely breathe.

I had a foreboding a few days prior to this incident and had consulted my astrologer. Pandit Dwarkanath had cautioned that I was going through a difficult phase. He had advised me that I shouldn't attend any functions, and that I should check with him if I had to attend. When Dinesh invited me to his party, I called Dwarkanath a couple of times to check if it would be alright for me to go to this event, but he didn't answer. And I thought to myself that since it was not an official function but a private party, there wouldn't be any harm in attending it. And then this *hungama* happened.

Picture my trauma when I got the letter. I was alone at home when it came. It's remarkable how I am always alone when I get momentous news. The lies mentioned in the letter shocked me as much as the order to resign. I rushed to show Dwarkanath the letter; he saw that it hadn't come through the *tappal*, the government's internal mail delivery system. As such it was a private letter, for the time being. He told me to go to the CM's house right away and return it to him.

When I went there, the family was about to leave for the wedding that I had also been invited to. Prema *Akka* saw that I was not dressed for it and asked, '*Neev madhuvege yaake barodilva*? (Why are you not coming to the wedding?)' She's an astute and perceptive person; even if she knows something, she never reveals it unless necessary.

I met S.M. Krishna and told him that if he wanted me to resign I would but asked him to tell me why he wanted my resignation.

He said, 'What you did was a disgrace to the cabinet.' I pointed out that he had known me from 1984 and asked if in all that time he had ever seen me drink. Why then would I misbehave as a Minister? He said that it wouldn't look good if the incident were to come out in the media; while he could contain the damage as long as the reports were confined to the vernacular media, he would not be able to keep me on as a minister if it were to come out in the national media. Fortunately for me, only two Kannada tabloids that made a living out of sensationalising and cooking up news, the *Lankesh Patrike* and *Agni*, published stories with all the made-up lies, '*avara koodalu hartha ithhu, avaru kuditha idhharu* (Her hair was flying, she was drinking).' But the mainstream media didn't make a big deal of it. S.M. Krishna took back his letter and I saved my berth. You can imagine the sleepless nights that I endured until the episode blew over. But I rejoiced too soon.

The Last Nail

In August, there was a public event for the inauguration of the Mekhri Circle underpass where many Ministers including the Chief Minister were present. I attended it too but as I had a prior appointment with the famous Dr Devi Shetty at the Narayana Hrudayalaya hospital, I sought the Chief Minister's permission to leave early. When I left the event though, Jaffer Sharief, the area MP and Union Railway Minister, who was on the dais, told S.M. Krishna that I was being disrespectful by leaving midway. This was also reported in *The Indian Express*. I saw the newspaper the next morning when I boarded a flight to Delhi and thought to myself that this was another black mark, adding to the pile of allegations against me.

When I was in Delhi, my eldest daughter Nishi called me and said, 'Mama did you get the news?' I countered, 'Have I lost my minister's post?' and she told me, 'You have lost the Medical Education portfolio and been demoted to Science & Technology.' When I lost my portfolio I was in Delhi and had, in fact, just finished meeting Sonia Gandhi. When the news came, she asked Ambika Soni to find out the reason. Ambika rang up the CM who told her that there were complaints against me for asking for too many medical college seats. She asked me to meet Sonia the next day. The evening I got the news, I took a hotel taxi at midnight and went to Ghulam Nabi Azad's house and to the AICC office on Ashoka Road to meet Oscar Fernandes to air my grievances. I howled and shrieked the whole night. Next morning my friend Tasu (Tasneem Mohammed) who had accompanied me on the trip told me to stop it, and get my act together. She asked me if I had lost my husband for me to become so hysterical. I calmed down after a while. Later I met Sonia with the letters from all the top leaders who had asked me to help their candidates get seats. My OSD had faxed all the request letters. Sonia told me, 'Don't make an issue of it. I'll look after you.' It was an empty promise. She did nothing. Nobody likes to rock the boat.

Karnataka state Congress president Allum Veerabhadrappa also announced that I was shifted because I had asked for the IT portfolio and that there were complaints from within the party about my performance in the Medical Education department. This time I didn't go to the CM. I didn't ask him to give me back my portfolio. I was absolutely livid and didn't want to talk to him.

To the press though, I echoed the party statement of the portfolios being the prerogative of the Chief Minister and announced that 'I am happy to be a part of S.M. Krishna's team. He has full confidence in me and hence, I have been entrusted with the responsibility of handling the Science and Technology portfolio. I have done full justice as Medical Education Minister and I am sure that I will handle the new portfolio with the same enthusiasm and zeal.'

Shifting me got the Congress some flak as it appeared that they were targeting the minorities. Just before demoting me, S.M. Krishna had sacked Civil Aviation Minister T. John (for his remarks that the 2001 earthquake in Gujarat 'was a punishment from God for the atrocities against Christians and other religious minorities'). My demotion and John's sacking were completely different issues but as usual politicians and the media try to add 2+2 and come up with 10!

I learned that if the Opposition gets a small issue, they rake it up and demand that the minister resign. And I also learnt another valuable lesson—the media can either make you or break you. I was the darling of the press at one time. That changed when S.M. Krishna's attitude changed towards me, thanks to my detractors.

When Life Gives You Lemons

Science & Technology was not a sought-after portfolio; in fact, nobody wanted it as it wasn't a lucrative portfolio. Most ministers lobby for money-making portfolios that have hefty budgets. I took it as a challenge and made something good out of it. When life gives you lemons, you can make refreshing lemonade. My policy was that what you do to your chair is important and not what your chair does for you.

I visited the prestigious Indian Institute of Science in the city, met scientists and educated myself. I had a long-term vision and all the issues that people have begun highlighting recently were taken up during my tenure. Now the whole world is talking about climate change and solar energy. I was talking about solar energy in 2002. The Union government is now talking about using ethanol as an alternative fuel. We began talking about energy from jatropha seeds

20 years ago. The seeds produce oil that is used in soaps, and energy for lighting and heating. Its biodiesel potential was being researched because the seeds contain 25 to 40 per cent oil. We started training people to extract and use it under the Mahatma Gandhi Institute of Rural Energy & Development; there were programmes in renewable energy for members of self-help groups and NGOs.

Back when I was the minister, I also initiated many projects and schemes to popularise rainwater harvesting. It was many years later though that it became a matter of priority. Only when people realised that water is not an infinite resource, did they begin to worry about a water crisis. I'm glad that the importance of rainwater harvesting has been realised by the government and the citizens.

The media reported these initiatives extensively, with *The Indian Express* giving good coverage:

> Nafees Fazal, minister of state for science and technology, said that the rainwater harvesting scheme which would be introduced in Bangalore next month, would later be extended to all gram panchayats.
>
> The scheme was expected to cover 25% of the domestic water needs in Bangalore and 50% of the industrial water requirement around the city.
>
> The adoption of rainwater harvesting technique and the use of solar energy is a simple mechanism.
>
> Stating that a lot of power was consumed for heating water, Mrs. Fazal said that efforts should be made to popularize the use of solar energy.
>
> Mrs. Fazal advised people to look out for new alternative forms of energies. The government will offer incentives to those who switch over to solar energy, she said.

She said that the Karnataka University at Dharwad had provided 100 acres land for setting up a science city there to inculcate a scientific temperament as pure science was on the wane.

Flying with Kalam

When A.P.J. Abdul Kalam was the Principal Scientific Advisor, as Minister for Science & Technology, I attended a meeting at the Indian Institute of Science (IISc) where Kalam was keen to take up the Brahm Prakash Memorial Chair. But the Institute was not keen; Kalam had a plan to meet one lakh children each year on the campus to inspire them to study science. But the IISc was a premier institute for higher learning and didn't want to bring in huge numbers of school kids. So they didn't give him the Chair.

Prof. Balakrishna 'Balki', a dear friend of Kalam and me, had arranged for lunch at 'Dakshin' restaurant, at the Windsor Manor. Hassan and Nishi also joined us.

After the lunch meeting, I took Kalam to meet the Chief Minister in the Vidhana Soudha. Just a month later Kalam became the President of India! Shortly after that, there was a science & technology programme in Mysuru which Kalam had to inaugurate and I had to address the conference. I had the opportunity to fly with him, the President, to Mysuru in a helicopter along with the Chief Minister. That's one of the most thrilling moments in my life. I was also very proud of myself because I gave an extempore speech in Kannada.

I have had a chequered career. I was a trendsetter in many ways and feel glad to have successfully implemented projects that have served the people well, in every post I held. We initiated computerization of hospital records and launched telemedicine and

I worked to get World Bank loans to upgrade government hospitals. I was also entrusted with the Karnataka Urban Infrastructure Development and Finance Corporation (KUIDFC) where I pushed for drinking water projects in Puttur (a city in Dakshina Kannada district) through a loan from the ADB, and the Kalasa-Banduri project to improve drinking water supply to Belagavi, Bagalkot, Dharwad and Gadag areas.

Some great initiatives didn't come through. In 2002, we began work on a 100-acre Science City, near the Bannerghatta National Park. The intent was to give pure science a fillip, as interest in it was waning. The Indian Space Research Organisation (ISRO) was to create a Space Museum on the campus too. We had a five-year plan to build it, but after political changes in the state, the project didn't materialise.

Medics in Villages

When I held the Medical Education portfolio, I wanted to focus on community medicine and I had pushed to make it mandatory for meritorious medical students to serve for three years in rural areas after their internship. These are students who have got merit seats and are being educated out of the taxpayers' money, and they should be of help to the rural poor. They take a vow to serve humanity before getting their degree. I pushed for the Karnataka government to make it mandatory for meritorious medicos to serve in the primary health centres and the primary health units for a minimum of three years after they complete their internship. Tamil Nadu and Maharashtra had already implemented this practice. I also thought this would give our medical students exposure to the ground reality, and this knowledge would help strengthen our healthcare system.

The medical students didn't object to the proposal either, but I didn't have time to amend the rule as I had been divested of my portfolio. I didn't need to go on study tours to other states or countries to formulate these policies; I used my foresight and common sense. Now, I am happy to see that there is a move to make merit seat students go to the villages for at least one year. It's taken 20 years for successive governments to implement what I had envisaged. Better late than never though!

I also initiated telemedicine to make expert healthcare available to people in different parts of the state. We connected major government hospitals in Bengaluru to hospitals in districts. Specialist doctors in Victoria, Kidwai, Bowring and similar hospitals would offer their expert consultation to patients from rural areas, who would be treated through the district hospitals. This was very effective and saved expenses that patients would incur by coming to Bengaluru to consult specialists.

Extraordinary Crises

There were two extraordinary crises that the government weathered during my time as a minister. They did not concern my departments in particular and I had no major role to play in the decisions about handling the crises. But I too was caught up in the emotional roller coaster rides that ensued. The first was the abduction of Dr Rajkumar by the sandalwood smuggler Veerappan, and the second was the Cauvery water dispute between Karnataka and Tamil Nadu.

The Hero & the Brigand

It was a case of real life overtaking and outdoing reel life. One of the biggest crises that the state government faced during my time as a minister was the kidnapping of the beloved matinee idol Dr Rajkumar by the dreaded brigand Veerappan. I still get goosebumps when I recall the incident.

Veerappan poached elephants for their ivory tusks and smuggled expensive and rare sandalwood trees from the forests of Karnataka, Tamil Nadu and Kerala. He had a ferocious reputation as a ruthless killer. Over 36 years, he's alleged to have killed almost 200 people, most of them police and forest officials. Having escaped from police custody very early in his career, he hid successfully in the thick forests. The bravest of brave officers headed the Special Investigation Teams but to no avail. The Centre even sent the Border Security Force to nab him, but he evaded all attempts to capture him.

Dr Rajkumar was a beloved icon of Kannadigas; a giant on the silver screen, off-screen, he was a simple man without any pretensions. In his golden years, his biggest joy was to build a new farmhouse opposite his ancestral house in Gajanur village. Gajanur or Dodda Gajanur, where Dr Rajkumar was born, is in Tamil Nadu, a few kilometres from the Karnataka border.

On 30 July, 2000, the darkest night of that month, the Amavasya, on the new moon night, Dr Rajkumar was in his farmhouse in Gajanur. He was watching TV with his wife, nephew and some other relatives when Veerappan and his henchmen walked in and asked Dr Rajkumar and three of his companions to accompany them and walk away. The abduction was accomplished as easily as that.

Starved for funds after his elephant poaching and sandalwood smuggling had been cut off, Veerappan had taken to raising money through kidnapping. In October 1997, he kidnapped two wildlife photographers Krupakar and Senani, and followed it up by kidnapping 15 tourists, including a scientist, from the Bandipur forest. When six senior forest officials set out in search of the tourists, Veerappan managed to kidnap them as well. However, he didn't harm any of them; he released everyone except the scientist, the photographers and the officials. He released them after a fortnight, following many rounds of negotiations. Such was the power he commanded from his forest hideout.

It became public knowledge after the matinee idol's abduction that the SIT (Special Investigation Team) set up to nab Veerappan had intelligence that Dr Rajkumar was on his radar. The actor's farmhouse in Gajanur abutted the wooded areas of the Sathyamangalam Wildlife Sanctuary, close to the brigand's hunting grounds. The police had impressed upon Dr Rajkumar and his family that he should inform them when he wanted to visit his farmhouse and that suitable protection would be given. On that particular visit, Dr Rajkumar had impulsively left without informing the police. Obviously, the brigand had kept close watch on his movements and upon realizing that the target was unprotected, picked him up. Later, the Supreme Court criticised the Tamil Nadu government for its 'unpardonable mistake' in its failure to depute police at Gajanur.

At that time though, to say the Karnataka government was shaken would be putting it mildly. The events of the fateful night of 30 July 2000 shook the state with the force of an earthquake. It seemed unimaginable but it was all too true.

Veerappan was illiterate and used a micro-cassette to communicate his demands. After the initial shock wore off, the opinion of the government was that he would negotiate a huge ransom. But as it turned out, Veerappan had gathered powerful friends; pro-Sri Lankan Tamil nationalists such as the Tamil National Retrieval Troops and the Tamil Nadu Liberation Army, both of which were banned in India, had joined Veerappan and set a new and more dangerous tone to the abduction. His list of demands included justice for Tamil Nadu in the Cauvery Water dispute, making Tamil the second official language of Karnataka and the release of some Tamil political prisoners who were in jail in Tamil Nadu.

As expected, there was a law and order situation in the state, with Dr Rajkumar's fans in Bengaluru and the old Mysuru areas being particularly volatile. There were anti-Tamil rumblings here and anti-Kannada murmurs in Tamil Nadu. The Chief Minister kept consulting his counterpart in Tamil Nadu, M. Karunanidhi, and tried everything in his power to bring the veteran actor home safely. Veerappan's chosen emissary was R. Gopal, the editor of the publication *Nakkeeran*, who played to the gallery after each visit to the jungle when he promised to return with the actor. Many hitherto unknown negotiators got involved, including one Dr Bhanu.

The expectations of a quick release had long since melted away and the entire gut-wrenching drama dragged on for over 100 days. Rajkumar was finally freed by Veerappan after 108 days. All of us in the government gave heartfelt thanks to God for his safe return. Had anything happened to him, I shudder to think of what would have transpired in the state.

The government did not make clear the exact circumstances of his release; the DGP and IG of Karnataka at that time, C. Dinakar, later wrote in his book that several consignments of cash were sent to Chennai to be given to Veerappan. He was sceptical about the exact amount that reached the brigand.

After the actor's release, the case against nine persons who were his alleged abductors dragged on for 18 years in a Tamil Nadu court. Rajkumar's family did not give evidence, and all were acquitted by the court. Meanwhile, in 2004, Veerappan was killed in an encounter with the SIT. In 2006, Dr Rajkumar died of a heart attack in his home in Bengaluru.

Water Wars

It was the summer of 2002, and the Cauvery Water Dispute had yet again set the state on the boil. The 805-km-long Cauvery originates in Talakaveri in Kodagu district, in the lush Western Ghats of Karnataka. From here, the river travels through Mysuru, Hassan and Mandya districts before wending its way through several districts of Tamil Nadu and joining the Bay of Bengal. It has several tributaries and the river basin also includes Kerala and Puducherry. The largely agrarian areas along its route depend heavily on the river for irrigation.

The sharing of the river waters is a potential landmine for any government on either side of the border. The dispute dates back to 1892 when the Madras Presidency and the Princely state of Mysore began arguing over sharing the river waters. The two signed a treaty and another one in 1924, after the intervention of the British colonialists. The agreement was about the usage of water from the Krishna Raja Sagara dam near Mysore. Neither side was happy with it but held the peace until the reorganisation of states took place after Independence.

Karnataka felt that the earlier agreement was skewed in Tamil Nadu's favour and demanded more water for its own use. It also pointed out that the agreement was outdated and hence could not be enforced. Tamil Nadu objected to any change. The Central government constituted a Tribunal in 1990 which took 16 long years to produce a final verdict. In the meantime, it issued interim orders about the sharing of the waters. The Central government also set up the Cauvery River Authority and the Cauvery Monitoring Committee.

All these bodies held many meetings as there were many contentious issues: the building of more dams, cultivating more land, droughts, and the demand for drinking water from growing cities. Matters usually came to a head when the rains failed and Tamil Nadu demanded water that Karnataka could not spare. So it was too in 2002.

The monsoons had failed in the south and reservoirs were empty. Tamil Nadu was adamant that Karnataka had to release its determined share of water. Karnataka pointed to the scarcity in its own dams and ruled out releasing any more water.

The Cauvery River Authority could not please either state though it tried to first please one and then the other. The Karnataka government defied the order to release the water as the protests in the Cauvery delta were building up and threatening to blow out of control. The Centre too asked Karnataka to release the water, while Tamil Nadu moved the Supreme Court. The Supreme Court ordered Karnataka on October 3 to obey the directives of the CRA and release water to Tamil Nadu.

I could well understand the dilemma of the Chief Minister. As a law-abiding head of government, he had to obey the highest court of the land but as the representative of the people of Karnataka, how could he release the water of life to a neighbour while our own people thirsted for it? We had suffered three successive years of drought and not a single person, cutting across party lines, would have agreed to its release.

It was an emotionally charged atmosphere. As Karnataka bravely refused to obey the orders of the Supreme Court, Tamil Nadu filed a contempt petition against Karnataka. Popular personalities in both states joined the issue; writers, poets, and artists lent their voices. Actors began overtaking politicians in political posturing. The film fraternity in both states shares a close bond, but the Cauvery water issue has tested it sorely many times.

It was a tense situation. Angry farmers had blocked roads, road and rail traffic between the two states and in the riparian areas were at a standstill, schools and colleges were closed, riot police stood guard at the reservoirs, and the toughest decision was to arrest the protesting farmers.

Caught between the devil and the deep blue sea, S.M. Krishna called for a protest march from Bengaluru to Mandya, the district worst affected by the water crisis. The entire cabinet and Congress workers walked the 100-km stretch in a protest 'padayatra'. I was energetic, fit and young enough to walk for 10 hours; we had an overnight break and continued the next morning in solidarity with the farmers. At a public meeting the Chief Minister announced, '*Ondu hani neeru koduvudilla* (We won't release a drop of water)'.

But behind the public posturing, we all knew that the Supreme Court's order had to be complied with. R.K. Dhawan also sent word through me that the Supreme Court order had to be obeyed and that water had to be released, as S.M. Krishna held a constitutional post of the Chief Minister of Karnataka. I conveyed this message to him. The SC had already cautioned that Karnataka was in contempt of court for deliberately disregarding the ruling. Hours before a crucial hearing in the Supreme Court to adjudicate on a petition filed by Tamil Nadu, the Karnataka cabinet decided to release the water.

As the world media watched and reported, hundreds of policemen in riot gear were deployed at the four main Cauvery reservoirs in the region to prevent angry farmers from storming the dams. As water again flowed across state lines the trouble subsided, if only for a while. It was an emotionally draining time for all of us in the government and I can only imagine the kind of pressure that the Chief Minister endured.

The Cauvery water issue simmered on and off for many more years before being resolved by the Supreme Court on 16 February 2018. In its final verdict on the dispute, the court allocated more water to the state of Karnataka. It also ordered the constitution of the Cauvery Water Management Authority (CWMA) and Cauvery Water Regulation Committee (CWRC).

S.M. Krishna's Kamaraj Plan*

In 2002, two-and-a-half years after he became the Chief Minister, S.M. Krishna wanted to revamp the council of ministers and quell dissent. Accordingly, all the ministers resigned to give him a free hand.

After that, we were extremely nervous, and we went through hell wondering who was in and who was out. Though Prema *Akka* is a big supporter of mine, her husband, the CM, would not tell her anything. We only knew that the next morning there would be a

* Kamaraj, a senior leader of the Indian National Congress, is regarded as a master political strategist. The Kamaraj Plan was a political plan formulated in 1963 that proposed that all senior Congress leaders should resign from their posts and devote all their energy to the revitalization of the Congress. The plan's intent was to stifle criticism of Prime Minister Nehru.

swearing-in ceremony at the Raj Bhavan where five new ministers would be inducted.

Nobody knew who they were. I went to find out the news from R.T. Narayan at the West End hotel. While I was there, my assistant Murthy called up and told me that I had got a phone call and that I was to go to the cabinet room. T.B. Jayachandra and A.M. Hindasgeri, who had also been ministers in the previous council, were also there in Narayan's room. Though neither of their assistants called with a similar message, Narayan, who was such a mischievous, meddlesome fellow, told them they should accompany me, even if they hadn't got the phone call.

The three of us went to Vidhana Soudha and moved to the cabinet room. Except for a minister and principal secretaries nobody can enter the cabinet room because of its sanctity. There were marshals at the entrance to the cabinet room, and when we reached there, one of them stopped us. He said that only I could enter but the other two couldn't as their names weren't on the list. Imagine the humiliation of my two former colleagues. The Chief Minister hadn't told them they were dropped; a marshal told them they were no longer ministers. The same thing had happened when I was removed from Medical Education. I had to find out from my daughter who got it from a journalist friend that I had been unceremoniously shifted. The humiliation we go through in politics is unbelievable. All is shining yellow gold from outside but this is a cruel game.

Early Polls

S.M. Krishna had weathered the kidnapping of Dr Rajkumar by Veerappan, and he had shown the people where his loyalties lay during the Cauvery crisis. He had done excellent work to showcase the capital city of Bengaluru as a modern, technologically advanced city, and initiated public-private cooperation through the Bangalore Agenda Task Force (BATF).

He could and should have easily lasted the whole of the five-year term comfortably. But in his wisdom, the Chief Minister called for elections eight months early. No doubt, he thought he would win with as good a margin as in 1999 and expected to continue as the CM with renewed strength. All the ministers were against the dissolving of the Assembly, but it was his prerogative as the Chief Minister to do so and he went ahead.

We all go into elections thinking we will win; nobody contests polls without being confident of victory. SMK's assessment was that the Congress would win. Two senior MPs, Manmohan Singh and Ambika Soni, met SMK in the Central Hall of Parliament and told him not to pre-empt the elections as the reports they had were very bad.

As events revealed, SMK had miscalculated badly in calling for early Assembly elections, coinciding with the Parliamentary elections in 2004. Political pundits have commented that 'when everything was going right for him, SMK committed *harakiri*'. They said that he didn't sense the disillusionment among the rural populace who found him too pro-urban.

This time, voters didn't vote in the same overwhelming majority for the Congress. For the Lok Sabha, Karnataka sent only eight MPs from the Congress, with BJP grabbing 18 seats and the Janata Dal (Secular) two seats. The Assembly results were sadder with the Congress's strength dwindling to less than half. But the voters didn't seem to like any of the political parties, and no party was able to win a majority. Although the BJP was the single largest party with 79 seats, political manoeuvring saw the Congress which had won 65 and the JD (S) with 58 seats forming a coalition government.

This was a first for Karnataka, and though the Congress gained power again, SMK had to cede the Chief Minister's post. Dharam Singh replaced SMK as the Chief Minister on 28 May 2004. The new Chief Minister wanted his own team, and my name didn't feature in the list of ministers. In with the new, out with the old! Not that Dharam Singh's cabinet lasted very long. In 2006, H.D. Kumaraswamy, JD(S) leader, pulled the rug from beneath his feet and announced a new alliance with the BJP. I could have predicted that JD(S) wasn't a trustworthy partner, had anyone bothered to ask me. Kumaraswamy was set on becoming Chief Minister and the grand old man of BJP in Karnataka B.S. Yediyurappa became the Deputy Chief Minister. This was the first taste of power for the BJP and set the ground for its speedy growth in the state.

Bowing Out

I served the remainder of my term as an MLC. Two years later, my term in the Legislative Council was over. I had been a minister for five years, MLC for seven years—a tenure of 12 years—and I wasn't ready to hang up my boots yet, not by a long shot. The fact remains that I never paid a *naya* paisa either to become an MLC or a Minister; I got whatever I did by sheer grit, hard work and luck of the draw, and the support of mentors, family and friends.

I had to go begging again. Like some other colleagues, I could have become the chairperson of some board, but I could not do so having been a minister. I had my heart set on getting back into the legislature. The sad reality is that all parties give all the losing seats to women; there are cogs within cogs in every party. Everybody wants their own *chamchas* (sycophants).

I tried many times to get a break somewhere. I tried to get the ticket to contest the Assembly elections from Jayamahal constituency in Bengaluru, but old man Jaffer wasn't letting go. Another reality is that there are very few seats where Muslims can win. If there is a likelihood of a Muslim winning, hey presto, the constituency is bifurcated.

In 2013, Bijapur, present-day Vijayapura, came to mind as it has a strong Muslim population and I thought I stood a good chance. Now, I had no choice but to fight an election. My dream was always to fight a direct election, but it was never fulfilled.

I started visiting Vijayapura frequently. Senior party leader Mallikarjun Kharge, currently the leader of the opposition in the Rajya Sabha, was most displeased. He told me that people from the south could not come to north Karnataka and fight an election, and that in any case the Congress supporters there would vote for a male candidate. Kharge had never forgiven me for my role in displacing Dharam Singh, his close friend, as Karnataka Congress party president and having SMK replace him. On a lighter note, we used to refer to the three strongmen of north Karnataka—H.K. Patil, Dharam Singh and Kharge—as 'set dosas' as they were very close to each other and formed a powerful clique.

Kharge was very friendly with M.B. Patil, a very wealthy politician with medical colleges in Vijayapura (he became a minister later). M.B. Patil did not want me there. He was apprehensive that if I won, I would get a ministerial berth as minority representative, and this would prevent him from becoming a minister as there can't be too many ministers from the same region. Patil and Kharge prevented me from getting the ticket. It was difficult for me to counter an influential local politician.

Politicians anticipate and play a long game. I was a mere pawn who got knocked off the chess board. It played out like this: I needed to build a base in Vijayapura and I had planned my moves. Elections to the local bodies were coming up and I decided to go to Vijayapura to campaign for the party candidates, as they could be of help in my own campaign if I were to get the Assembly ticket. To cover my expenses, I had taken cash that I had withdrawn from Karnataka Apex Bank, from its branch at the Vidhana Soudha. I withdrew Rs 1,50,000 and I had the receipt with me.

I was resting in my room in Vijayapura when 10 policemen and women barged into my room without even announcing themselves. They said it was a raid as they had got a complaint that I had brought cash to bribe voters. I showed them the receipt for the cash and pointed out that the money was for my personal expenses. I had driven there in my car and I was going to stay for 10 days. I had my gunman and my driver. I had to pay for the fuel, our stay, and such expenses. How could that be construed as bribe money?

I was furious and complained to the Election Commission. But at that point, I was powerless. The police seized the money and my car. To add to my mortification, I had to return to Bengaluru in a car arranged by Patil. This humiliation was unjustified.

I had planned my moves, and even begged, but none of it was of any use. After my disappointment in Vijayapura, I did not want to ask for anything. I was dejected and disappointed. I bowed out of the race, for good.

Failure & Depression

Power is the most attractive aphrodisiac, and we politicians pine without it. After I failed in getting the ticket for the Vijayapura Assembly seat, I felt hollow. My self-worth diminished and I went into depression. It was an awful feeling. I turned to Dr K.G. Das, who was both my doctor and confidant. He said to me, 'Diamonds don't crumble; they are sharp and cut others. You are a diamond. To regain your strength and confidence, get hold of yourself and forget politics for some time. It's a question of mind over matter, and you will surely overcome this setback.'

S.M. Krishna was equally taken aback that I was crumbling. He told me, 'Nafees, how many women have been ministers? You will go to your grave as an ex-minister. Get negativity out of your system and see the positive side of your achievements.' Both SMK and Dr Das helped me get through one of the most horrid phases of my life and by the grace of Allah and my prayers I managed to pull through it. I realised there's more to life than my career; I am very fortunate to have a loving family, a handful of loyal and affectionate friends, and many well-wishers. I promised myself therefore to enjoy a rich and full life by repaying my debt to society.

We are all human and do crumble when we face adversity. People in public life are under greater stress because of the constant glare of publicity and the high expectations that the public has of them, and they have of themselves. At such times, one should reach out to friends and well-wishers and take strength and courage. Mental well-being is not to be ignored nor is there any shame in seeking help to overcome depression.

CENTRAL HALL

As a minister one enjoys many privileges, and perhaps one that I enjoyed the most was the access my position gave me to enter the Central Hall of Parliament. It was an awe-inspiring experience to be in the mecca of politics. The aura is unparalleled and the very air breathes of power. I was privileged to meet all the top Union ministers and MPs of my party as everybody comes there for a coffee break.

Words of caution or encouragement, promises made and broken—this hall has witnessed the making and breaking of parties and careers.

4

Gender & Religion @ Work

WOMEN ARE NOT natural enemies of other women. That's just a myth made up by men. The reality of my lived experience is that it's always been women who recognised the spark in me, gave me opportunities, encouraged me, protected me, and fought for me.

Margaret Alva supported me from the very beginning and continued to do so at my lowest ebb. Whatever she promised me, she fulfilled. Prema Krishna has been a good friend and ally; she's really like the elder sister I never had, and she's stepped in to help me many times. At the national level, Ambika Soni supported me when I was a minister; she was the general secretary of the Congress in charge of Karnataka. We became close when we went to Bellary to campaign for Mrs Sonia Gandhi. I have seen Margaret and Ambika help several women like me in politics.

Sexist Attitudes

As for men, it was a different matter. They looked at my gender and religion and judged me; sadly, very few saw my ability and dedication. Whether it was my western style education or the fact that I had a privileged life or that I refused to change the way that I spoke or dressed, I didn't fit the archetypal Muslim housewife. And that was cause for concern among Muslim politicians of my time. My glamorous image went against the grain of my critics. I was a pawn in the game of politics and due to the manipulations of the Muslim men, my career had a premature death.

I come from an apolitical family and establishing myself in politics was very difficult. When I joined politics, I reached out for political guidance to the Congress stalwart, C.K. Jaffer Sharief. He reigned supreme as the MP from Bangalore North Lok Sabha and as a Union Minister. Sharief was courteous and friendly to me, but he had his reservations about my pursuit of politics. He, like other conservative Muslim men, felt that Muslim women should be confined to the home, as dutiful housewives, or remain low-key and occupy themselves with charitable affairs. My image as a fashionable progressive woman was also a drawback. What did Jaffer do for me? He didn't help me and I was defeated in the corporation elections. He also didn't help my efforts to get a ticket to the Assembly.

Trying to juggle my fledgling political career and my role as a wife and mother was difficult. It became more so after I contested the local bodies' election (which I lost by 67 votes). But I was sure this is what I wanted and never wavered in my determination to be a successful politician.

Eight months after I became a minister, I was up for renomination to the Legislative Council. To my consternation, I found that my critics had prepared a dossier on me and given it directly to Sonia Gandhi, bypassing the Chief Minister. They alleged that I was smoking in the Vidhana Soudha. I am not a lunatic and I know what behaviour is appropriate. How could I sit in Vidhana Soudha and smoke? Mrs Gandhi put the dossier in front of SMK and asked him if the allegations were true. SMK told her that they were all fabricated by my detractors and ensured that I was renominated.

I was shocked to see that my detractors would stoop to such levels. Every action of mine was amplified. A lot of fake news was planted about me. These men really took me to the cleaners. I have suffered a lot of humiliation. Like the time I was accused of dancing at Dinesh Gundu Rao's party. The double standards and hypocrisy was blatant. Nobody questioned the host. There were so many male party leaders at the same party who were drinking, and some of them were also dancing. Nobody made an issue of their behaviour, but I was singled out and falsely accused simply because I was a woman.

B.S. Yediyurappa, BJP leader and former Chief Minister of Karnataka, was an MLC when I was a minister. He picked on me and tried to implicate me in the Telgi case. Like most men, he probably found me very abrasive and fiery and could not tolerate my guts.. When he tried to link my husband in the Telgi case, I made a public demand via the media that he should produce proof to back his allegations, but of course he had none. Perhaps, the issue got ample publicity because I was a Minority woman leader.

Media Bias

The yellow rags in the media, the cheap little tabloids, were particularly cruel to me. They referred to me as 'Nafees Fossil'—I was not a senior citizen when I was a minister, and took pride in staying fit and alert, physically and mentally. Yet, such derogatory remarks were hurtful and I was singled out yet again because of my gender. Journalists, especially male journalists, focus on the appearances of women instead of their achievements. This is a gender bias that is evident even today in the media, which pillories and objectifies women without a qualm.

Close Encounter

In 1994, Basavarajeshwari Jahagirdar, the MP of Ballari (earlier Bellary) and Union Minister, requested a very powerful Muslim Union Minister from Karnataka and me to campaign for her son and garner Muslim votes in her constituency in her son's favour. I decided to go there for two days.

The train from Bengaluru to Ballari was at night and I got into a salon reserved for the minister. A friend of the minister, a very nice gentleman, Venkateshwar, was also travelling with him, and after a while, he went to his compartment to sleep. I was taken aback when the minister suddenly drew close to me and touched me. I was livid and started cursing him and he exited the compartment.

At two in the morning when the train stopped at Guntakal Junction, between Bengaluru and Ballari, the minister jumped off the train. The railway guard on special duty to the minister informed us that the minister had departed with his paraphernalia. We were in a state of shock. I advised Venkateshwar that we better get down at the next station and return to Bengaluru. We learnt that a train from Ballari to Bengaluru was coming after 15 minutes. So we both jumped off the train and spent half an hour on the platform; it was December and it was extremely cold. When we got onto the train, we asked to be directed to the salon. The guard told us that the minister was there, headed to Bengaluru too! Venkateshwar felt it would be better if we didn't disturb him at that hour and we found other seats for ourselves. In the morning, I went to meet the minister and asked why he had got off the train in the night without informing either of us. He said to me, 'I had to ease myself!' It is a cruel joke that a railway salon has no toilet for the minister!

Casting Couch

Several people have asked me if there's a casting couch in politics. I always counter by asking, 'Why would politics be different than any other sector?' It's a known fact that certain women have risen to prominence because they have the attention and protection of powerful men. Some of these could be in physical relationships with their sugar daddies and some may have used their position to do the work they set out to do. I will neither judge these women nor belittle them. They are also victims of a patriarchal system.

I remember that at one of my lowest points, after I had already spent 14 years waiting for a break, I asked my dear friend R.K. Dhawan whether I was not rising in politics because I wasn't playing bedroom politics. He cautioned me that there was no turning back from such a path. 'They will pass you around till you become a whore,' he said. It was a warning I took to heart. Pointing to my palm, he said, '*Idhar likha hai toh banenge* (If it's written in my fate, I would get a break in politics).'

Exceptional Men

Dhawan comes under the category of a few exceptional men I have known; not all men are bad. Apart from my dearest husband Hassan, who's been a blessing and a rock in my life, there have been some men whom I met in the world of politics who have been friends, philosophers, and guides in my profession.

In early 1980, Indira Gandhi had just been sworn in as Prime Minister and I wanted to meet her. Jaffer Sharief had become the Minister of State for Railways and I asked him to introduce me as I had worked so hard for his campaign. The only way anyone could get to her was through Dhawan, her trusted personal secretary. Sharief called Dhawan and told him that he was sending me to meet him.

Dhawan was in such an influential position that even powerful chief ministers would compete to get into his chambers before meeting Madam. I remember my first meeting with him in Indira Gandhi's Safdarjung Road office. There he was suited and booted with a tie. He was sitting with a packet of Dunhill cigarettes, smoking. I looked at him and I commented, '*Aap kitne lucky hai* (you are so lucky)' and he asked what I meant. I indicated his cigarette and he promptly offered me one. In fact, smoking became our bond. I know it is politically incorrect to admit to smoking these days, but I have no qualms in saying that I smoke; I am leading my life, and I am not bothering anyone else.

Dhawan and I took to each other at our very first interaction. Whenever I went to Delhi, which was very often, I would always ring up Dhawan*ji*. He became a family friend and used to call me 'Sweetu'. Several times during my career, I sought his advice, though I didn't always heed it. He played a very important role in my life. He also advised me never to take on my superiors, as I wouldn't be able to survive the clash. This was a prescient warning, as years later when S.M. Krishna divested me of my portfolio, I remembered this piece of valuable advice and calmed down. He was kind to me; he was a charming person with a very fine personality. It was sad that he was implicated and investigated by the Thakkar Commission in Indira Gandhi's assassination. Indira*ji* was his golden goose; he derived all power only because of his proximity to her. Why then would he want her dead? I was glad when Rajiv Gandhi cleared him of the charges of involvement in Indira Gandhi's assassination and I was devastated when he died in August 2018.

Aiyar & Me

The redoubtable Mani Shankar Aiyar was another person who became a good friend. One morning I was waiting to see Prime Minister Rajiv Gandhi, standing in line along with others outside his house for the general darshan. Mani was chatting with another MP, Jayanthi Natarajan. I didn't recognise him but I heard them chatting in Tamil. Mani admired women and I saw both of them looking at me. Jayanthi asked him in Tamil, '*Inda ponnu koodu yevala doora poh irkere*? (How far have you gone with this girl?).' He laughed and said '*Mukal vasi achi* (three-fourth of the way).'

I was shocked and angry. I went up to them and said, 'Excuse me, I am from Tamil Nadu and understand what you are saying. Why are you talking shit about me? I don't even know who you are.' He was very apologetic and we became friends later. Thanks to Mani, who was a special assistant to the PM, I had the opportunity to be in Rajiv Gandhi's motorcade during his visits.

After that first encounter, Mani was never improper with me. His mentality was, 'Why should I chase you? If you are not interested then let us remain good friends.' Not all men are made that way.

But for people like Mani, consent is very important. We have stayed friends till today.

SMK – My Benefactor

S.M. Krishna was the one who made me a minister and I am eternally grateful to him for it. I remember his words, 'Nafees, this is an achievement nobody can ever take away from you. Once you become a minister, your name will go down in history.' Earlier, when he became KPCC president, he made me the vice-president of the Karnataka Congress Committee. Because of my closeness with his wife, I had free access to his house and could walk in at any time. Despite the ups and downs in politics, I have always admired and respected him. He helped me immensely.

When he was the Governor of Maharashtra, S.M. Krishna hosted my entire family at the historic Raj Bhavan in Mumbai, during the wedding of R.V. Deshpande's son. It was a priceless experience. When S.M. Krishna was the External Affairs Minister of India, he sent Hassan and me on a goodwill pilgrimage for Haj. We were treated with great courtesy throughout our stay, which began with being received by Indian Ambassador Hamid Ansari at the Jeddah airport. It was a very special visit.

The person who made me realise that SMK was indeed my well-wisher was Vincent George, Sonia Gandhi's personal assistant. I had blamed SMK for taking away the Medical Education portfolio from me and assigning a portfolio which at the time was perceived to be less important. It was George who told me that SMK had pleaded D.K. Shivakumar's and my cases with folded hands before Sonia and ensured that we both were inducted into the council of ministers.

George, like Dhawan before him, controlled access to the party president and has always been kind and courteous to me.

Unfair Treatment

But these men are exceptional. For the most part, I think men like to suppress women because they want to show that they are superior. That is my understanding of the situation. I realised as a young girl that Muslim men are the biggest MCPs and my opinion was reinforced in politics.

There have been countless times that I experienced gender discrimination. All the years that I have put in politics, as a legislator and a minister, have no meaning. I am not consulted, let alone involved, even in the selection of candidates for civic elections for wards in my area. The media has reported about such noticeable lapses. The *Deccan Chronicle* noted on 11 August 2015 that 'Former minister Nafees Fazal seems to be upset with the party for not consulting her over the selection of candidates for the BBMP polls for the Wards falling in the Pulikeshi Nagar assembly segment. Party sources said that she was not invited to the selection committee meeting too'.

I was invited to campaign across Karnataka, especially in Muslim-dominated areas, before the Assembly elections in 2013. I travelled with other party leaders to Gulbarga, Bidar, and other districts. But Naseer Ahmed, MLC and former minister, would not even give me a chance to speak at any of the meetings. I had to just keep mum there. I could not have imagined anyone being so petty or nasty. I am a valuable asset as the first and so far the only Muslim woman to be a minister in the south of India. The Muslim male politicians especially can't stomach my achievements as a Muslim woman.

When Siddaramaiah became the Chief Minister, I asked him why he was keeping me in the political wilderness. He replied cryptically, '*Amma*, leaders from your own community are not endorsing your candidature.' I have cursed all of them. As an astrologer once told me, '*Amma nimma shaapa Chamundeswari thara* (your curse is like Goddess Chamundeswari's curse).'

Siddaramaiah and Rahul Gandhi talked a lot about women's empowerment, but the reality is that Muslim women are being denied a voice, and the support is only for our male counterparts, who view progressive women like me as competition and resent our growth. Siddaramaiah joined the Congress in 2006, after being expelled from the JD(S) by Deve Gowda in 2005. Being a newcomer, he did not recognise senior Congress workers.

Apparently, not only were the Muslim men against me, but men in general within the Congress worked against me. When I was the minister for Science & Technology, and Indian Systems of Medicine/ Homoeopathy, Jagadish Shettar of the BJP was the Leader of the Opposition. One day, he rang me up and asked me to nominate one of his followers to the homeopathy board. I asked him how he could ask me to do this when the Opposition kept hounding for my resignation. I was sad to hear his answer, '*Naan yen madli, nimma pakshadavare helikoduthare.* (What can I do? Your party people are prompting us).' My own party people were telling Jagadish Shettar to ask for my resignation. All ministers go through hardship; it is worse if you are a woman and outspoken – you are disliked and your growth obstructed by your own party members.

Whether you are rich or poor, whichever community you may come from, women are the underdogs and are subjected to character assassination. Even Sonia Gandhi was not spared; her detractors morphed her photos trying to project her in a poor light. Motivated campaigns and discrimination against women in politics happens all over the world, not just in India. Look at how Hillary Clinton was deprived of the Presidency of the USA by motivated attacks. Media reports have mentioned that Kamala Harris is facing a rough time as the first female Vice-President of the USA.

Women have to persevere and prevail over motivated personal attacks. My advice to women with political ambitions and others who are career oriented is to develop a thick skin. Ignore the slurs. Don't be despondent or throw in the towel. Be courageous and face adversities.

Women can overcome obstacles if they support each other. In our country, women have held high political office – of president, prime minister, chief minister, members of parliament, party and coalition presidents. They could have used their positions to help women more than they did.

At the risk of sounding immodest, I would like to cite a few ways that I helped women merely to demonstrate that if one has the interest, it's not difficult to smooth the way. I helped many women in our party to get tickets to contest the Bangalore City Corporation elections; I also helped them with funding to fight the election. With my intervention, a good number of women became chairpersons on boards and corporations. At my request, Chief Minister S.M. Krishna nominated two women as MLCs and a few got Assembly seats.

My biggest achievement as a minister was upgrading the burns ward in Victoria Hospital and rendering justice to victims. Women who were victims of dowry harassment came in large numbers with 50 to 90 per cent burns. I released funds to upgrade the burns ward.

The common complaint by the families of the burn victims was that the Janata stove had burst while cooking. This was far from the truth. In order to render justice to the dying victims and to book cases against their in-laws for dowry harassment, we appointed a district magistrate or equivalent authority to take the dying declaration of burn victims.

Since I was a member of the Congress party, I was able to achieve my goals of helping the destitute. I use my office to help many women, especially the downtrodden and destitute. Indira Gandhi had many programmes for the poor and the needy which I took up on a war footing. Hordes of women used to come to my office in Cunningham Road for old age pensions and widow pensions and I used to monitor their applications until they got their dues.

I used my good offices to help aggrieved women to file their complaints against harassment and torture. Some needed psychiatric help and others needed counselling. We set up a helpline in the police commissioner's office in Bengaluru for women to come forward with their complaints. Many NGOs participated in this programme and we were able to render help.

I visited government Urdu schools to inspect the hygiene and conditions of the buildings, and I saw to it that their problems with drinking water facilities, etc. were redressed.

Even in trying to render social service, I faced gender discrimination. The BBMP (Bruhat Bengaluru Mahanagara Palike), which is otherwise very generous in allotting land to big players for commercial purposes like the Garuda Mall, wouldn't give me a small piece of land in Shivajinagar where I wanted to put up a night shelter for destitute women. I fought to get the land but it was denied to me.

Widening Gender Gap

It's a matter of grave concern that according to the World Economic Forum's Global Gender Gap Report 2021 India ranks 140th among 156 countries. Our country slipped 28 places from 2020 to 2021, becoming the third-worst performer in South Asia with only Pakistan and Afghanistan ranked below. The report noted that India, which has a population of 0.65 billion women, widened the gender gap by 3 per cent. Most of the decline was in the political empowerment subindex, where India regressed 13.5 percentage points. There was a significant decline in the number of women ministers from 23.1 per cent in 2019 to 9.1 per cent in 2021. It seems all the more urgent now that political parties should arrive at a consensus and pass the Women's Reservation Bill.

Women's Reservation Bill

Looking at the larger picture, past my own experiences, I don't see any party being cognizant of women's rights. As in other spheres, gender discrimination continues to exist in politics. No further evidence is necessary than the fact that the Women's Reservation Bill continues to languish after three decades.

This Bill proposed to amend the Constitution to reserve one-third of all seats in the Lower House of Parliament of India, the Lok Sabha, and in all state legislative assemblies, for women. It was first introduced in the Lok Sabha in September 1996. Though successive governments have gone through the motions of introducing it and political parties had promised to do so in their election manifestoes, the Bill has never found the support that it needs to become law.

As per the Bill, 33 per cent of seats are to be reserved for women on a rotational basis. The seats would be determined by a draw of lots in such a way that a seat would only be reserved once in every three consecutive general elections.

It has never passed the Lok Sabha as male politicians consider women to be a threat to their position. Until the Bill is enacted, all the posturing of political parties is a mockery of women's equality. It is the duty of every female politician, irrespective of the party she belongs to, to insist that this should be made a priority.

Just look at the wonderful work that women are doing at the panchayat and municipal levels – the rise of Sampatiya Uikey, the tribal leader from Madhya Pradesh, from grassroots worker to Member of Parliament, is just one case in point. Women have been breaking glass ceilings in different areas of work. In the corporate world, they have been heading billion-dollar companies—Indra Nooyi was the Chairperson & CEO of Pepsico and featured on several lists of world's most powerful women; Kiran Mazumdar Shaw founded and led Biocon to the biotech giant it is today. Be it Arundhati Bhattacharya, the first woman Chair of the State Bank of India who now heads the Indian operations of Salesforce, the global SaaS giant, or Dr Soumya Swaminathan, Chief Scientist at the World Health Organization, it's a matter of rejoicement that there are several such women leaders these days.

A just and inclusive society needs women in power. I am happy that leadership opportunities for Muslim women are expanding today. They are not bound by the regressive notions of past generations about women's abilities, positions and roles. Anyone can aspire to be anything or do anything – age, religion and gender are no bar. I hope that the Women's Reservation Bill is enacted into law; this is a long overdue step that would transform governance in India.

What would also help women pursue political aspirations is the creation of more convivial infrastructure. Women candidates and their supporters dread the lack of clean and safe amenities like toilets while campaigning, the location of the venues for political rallies and the timing (rallies are generally held late at night).

Uniform Civil Code & CAA

I think the Uniform Civil Code is a welcome move. I had earlier opposed it but, after due consideration, I feel it is important to mainstream all minorities and remove the disparities. I am quite clear about that and this is my stand on the two important issues: the Uniform Civil Code and the Citizenship Amendment Act.

The Citizenship Amendment Bill makes distinctions between Muslim refugees who are not welcome and Hindus, Christians, Sikhs, and other non-Muslims who are welcome. Muslims never feel accepted because of such disparity in treatment.

We are one nation and have to be one people. We have too many divisions already, and we need to have unity without disparity between majority and minority. The Uniform Civil Code has to apply to all including Hindu Undivided Families.

One Law, One Nation

The Hindu Succession Act, which applies to Hindus, Buddhists, Jains, and Sikhs in India, grants Hindu women an equal share in the ancestral property by birth. The Supreme Court has also given them retrospective succession rights. When Hindu women are entitled to inherit ancestral property, why can't Muslim women? We Muslim women are victims in such cases. *Nana*, my grandfather, though he was well versed in Sharia and was also Sheriff of Madras, did great injustice to his daughters and their descendants. According to the Sharia, a male gets two shares, a girl one share, and the wife gets one-eighth. *Nana* was a billionaire and created a private wakf (trust) to secure his many properties for his heirs. Twenty-five years after he set up the wakf, eight days after my birth, he introduced an explanation that by heirs he meant only males and their descendants.

He's a sinner in the eyes of Allah as many female descendants in the family are going through hard times due to paucity of funds. Seeing my cousins suffer financially, I feel one law and one nation is not a bad idea. The Muslim clergy and *mullahs* who don't brook any interference in the Sharia should be speaking up about this flagrant violation.

I have been denied my inheritance simply because I am a woman. I still can't fathom why the grandfather who loved me so much and treasured me as his princess could be so unjust. When I was born, he appeared to have realised that his first grandchild was a girl and promptly excluded all the descendants of his daughters from his will, thus ensuring that I would never get the benefit of our family's sizeable estate.

I am fortunate that I did not need his money but many cousins, children of my mother's sisters, have suffered because of this unfair treatment. As it turned out, two important men who were pillars of our community, neither the Sheriff of Madras nor the Sharief of Bangalore, were *sharif* (noble) when it came to giving women their due!

Mainstreaming Minorities

The Quran Sharief contains verses that support the role of women in politics. This includes its mention of the Queen of Sheba, who represented a ruler who consulted with and took important decisions on behalf of her people. Further, the Hadith (which contains the reported sayings of Prophet Muhammad (peace be upon him) provides numerous examples of women having public leadership roles. Many Muslim countries like Bangladesh, Pakistan, Turkey, Indonesia, etc. have had Muslim women lead their country; Benazir Bhutto, Khaleda Zia, Sheikh Hasina and Megawati Sukarnoputri to name a few.

However, self-appointed organisations like the All India Muslim Personal Law Board (AIMPLB) have usurped the power to interpret the Quran Sharief and have been dictating terms. The AIMPLB was formed in 1973 by a motley group during Indira Gandhi's time as she wanted the Muslim votes. These fundamentalists, who have been given importance by the Congress, are very regressive. In 2015, they led a nationwide protest against *surya namaskar* and yoga, calling them anti-Islam. I am a practicing Muslim who has performed Haj four times and says *namaz* five times a day, but I have been doing yoga for 30 years. I have observed a similarity between the postures in the *surya namaskar* and *namaz*. In a survey done in 2015 by the Bharatiya Muslim Mahila Andolan (BMMA), they said that 95 per cent of the women surveyed did not know of the AIMPLB and that young Muslims in both rural and urban areas did not agree with their views and found it medieval and regressive.

The AIMPLB is behaving like the *Khap panchayats* (caste or clan-based groups prevalent in Haryana) who are a law unto themselves. These *maulvis* and *mullahs* don't have the authority to issue *fatwas* (statements or orders from an Islamic religious leader). I have called them out time and again for their regressive stand. It is high time that the AIMPLB is dismantled for being unconstitutional – as they are working against the rights of Muslim women.

The AIMPLB has often used *fatwas* to control women and take shelter behind absolutely baseless interpretations of the Quran Sharief. *Fatwas* (from the Arabic word for explanations or clarifications) are, technically, legal opinions on matters of Islamic law, practice or convention issued by recognised religious authorities; in other words, it is an expert opinion. In practice, *fatwas* are often issued by publicity-seeking *mullahs* for political purposes by misusing their authority to make them sound like diktats or orders, which they are not. *Fatwas* have no legal standing and cannot be enforced by use or threat of force and nor can people be forced to accept them as absolute or binding.

Look at the *fatwas* issued by the Darul Uloom Deoband in Uttar Pradesh (India's largest Islamic seminary). One *fatwa* says that no police report can be filed against the father-in-law who allegedly raped his daughter-in-law. According to the *fatwa*, the father-in-law could have been blamed only if there had either been a witness to the case or the victim's husband had endorsed the victim's allegation. Another *fatwa* asked a 19 -year-old Muslim woman to accept the rapist father-in-law as her real husband and divorce her husband. The list continues with grave to bizarre *fatwas*. On 22 October 2017, we saw a *fatwa* prohibiting women from cutting their hair or shaping their eyebrows and posting pictures of themselves or their family on social media. *The Deccan Chronicle* reported my views under the headline, '*Fatwas* are interpretations of Quran Sharief, not diktats'. I will elaborate on that report.

The Deoband *fatwa* quoted the Quran Sharief, which says one cannot modify their appearances (happily omitting the fact that this holds good both for men and women). Men and women in some Islamic countries wear jeans and colour their hair, so why should their counterparts in India, a secular nation, not do the same here? Sheikhdoms in the Middle East in fact have photographs of the rulers in every public office and space. Why then a *fatwa* against photographs?

I maintain that the people who issue *fatwas* have their own ways of interpreting verses from the Quran Sharief and differ with each other at times. Some of the things that the Deoband *fatwa* asks people to avoid doing are impractical in the 21st century. The holy verses condemn idolatry and have asked people not to draw human figures, but this ban for example cannot be extended to photographs. We must also keep in mind that *fatwas* are never diktats.

There is no mention either, in the Quran Sharief, about women covering their faces entirely - this is prohibited at Mina and Arafat where men and women stand shoulder to shoulder as the Haj is performed. Only the hair needs to be covered in keeping with the holy verses. The regressive practices we see now have been introduced by the mullahs.

The Quran Sharief does not differentiate between a man and a woman in the way these organisations, like the AIMPLB, and *mullahs* claim in the name of Islam. My daughters wear jeans and dress according to the times – I don't see this as a violation of the Quran Sharief. There is room for choice and progressive interpretation in the Quran Sharief using the main principles of Islam as one's guiding light – kindness (to people and animals), charity, forgiveness, honesty, patience, justice, respecting parents and elders, keeping promises, and controlling one's anger, love of God and those God loves, love of his messenger (Muhammad) and of believers. We are asked to use wisdom, courage, temperance and justice as our values on which to base our actions and thoughts.

Too much focus is given to Islamist terror outfits like Lashkar-e-Taiba (LeT) and Jaish-e-Mohammad (JeM or the Army of Mohammed) that claim themselves to be representatives of Islam. Let me be very clear, extremism and terrorism for any reason and in any form is absolutely wrong and we should have zero tolerance for it.

These terror groups do not reflect the principles of Islam. They use the platform of religion to gain recognition for their self-serving ends, and create unnecessary divisions in society. Their actions have destroyed the very community they say they want to protect. All Muslims everywhere are paying a heavy price for their unconscionable actions.

And why are the same *mullahs* who oppose the emancipation of women given air time on news channels? *Mullahs* want publicity, and the anchors, who act like feudal lords, call them on their shows. This sort of media attention puts Islam in a bad light. Terror outfits like LeT and JeM are not part of Islam, as terrorism has no name or religion. We don't consider terrorists to be Muslims as they are against the preaching of our Prophet Muhammad (peace be upon him). They bring a bad name to the whole religion. I am of the opinion that TV channels propagate a bias when they debate these issues with these self-serving representatives. Most channels lean towards the right wing. One of them is even being funded by a right-wing politician, so can we expect anything else?

Media can play a critical role in mainstreaming the views of progressive Muslims. Our interpretation of Islam and understanding also deserves equal airtime. Media should provide opportunities for this section to share their perspectives too, to aid nation-building and in keeping with the very idea of India – unity with diversity.

Triple Talaq

Talaq, talaq, talaq – these are the three words that send shivers down the spine. I have come across thousands of cases where Muslim men have misused this unilateral power to divorce their wives. Pronouncing these words lightly on the phone, in text messages, e-mails, video calls, and even on WhatsApp, heartless husbands have cast wives and children out of their family homes, rendering them destitute.

Hence, I am firmly behind the Muslim Women (Protection of Rights on Marriage) Act, 2019. I believe that the triple *talaq* is one of the most regressive practices and it's shameful that it has been allowed to go on as long as it did in India. It has been banned in over 20 Muslim countries and India hadn't been able to follow suit because of organisations such as the AIMPLB.

My point is that if you harp on Sharia law, then you should follow it all the way. Instant *talaq* is not in keeping with the Sharia. If you must harp on it, follow it all the way! Why only subject a woman to it? The Sharia says that a person who commits murder should be beheaded and anyone who commits theft should have their hands chopped off. Sharia law also says adulterers should be stoned to death. Are we following this today? If they really want to safeguard Islamic law, they should fight for equal implementation of the Sharia for both men and women. In Saudi Arabia, a Prince has been lashed and another was executed for breaking the Sharia law that is practised there. *Talaq* should be performed in the Quranic way, according to Surah At-Talaq. Let me make clear that I'm not asking for the implementation of Sharia in India. It is the diktats given by incompetent people like *mullahs* and *maulvis*, most of who are not well versed with the teachings of the Quran Sharief and are misguiding Muslims

The Congress party's refusal to back the Muslim Women (Protection of Rights on Marriage) Bill was one of the reasons that firmed up my decision to leave it. The one thing that I admire about Prime Minister Narendra Modi is his stand on triple *talaq*. I had requested him to disband the AIMPLB. I was positive that Modi*ji* would not interfere or nullify the triple *talaq* judgment like Rajiv Gandhi did in the Shah Bano case in 1986. I was unequivocal that the Act banning triple *talaq* was for gender justice, equity and empowerment—something that Muslim women desperately needed.

August 1, the day that the Act came into force, is observed as 'Muslim Women's Rights Day' and it's noteworthy that there has been a considerable decline in the number of triple *talaq* cases after the law came into effect in 2019.

For the benefit of the readers, here is the gist of this milestone legislation, courtesy PRS India.

- The Bill makes all declarations of *talaq*, including in written or electronic form, to be void (i.e. not enforceable in law) and illegal. It defines *talaq* as *talaq-e-biddat* or any other similar form of *talaq* pronounced by a Muslim man resulting in instant and irrevocable divorce. *Talaq-e-biddat* refers to the practice under Muslim personal laws where pronouncement of the word '*talaq*' thrice in one sitting by a Muslim man to his wife results in an instant and irrevocable divorce.

- **Offence and penalty:** The Bill makes declaration of *talaq* a cognizable offence, attracting up to three years' imprisonment with a fine. (A cognizable offence is one for which a police officer may arrest an accused person without a warrant.) The offence will be cognizable only if information relating to the offence is given by: (i) the married woman (against whom *talaq* has been declared), or (ii) any person related to her by blood or marriage.

- The Bill provides that the Magistrate may grant bail to the accused. The bail may be granted only after hearing the woman (against whom *talaq* has been pronounced), and if the Magistrate is satisfied that there are reasonable grounds for granting bail.

- The offence may be compounded by the Magistrate upon the request of the woman (against whom *talaq* has been declared). Compounding refers to the procedure where the two sides agree to stop legal proceedings and settle the dispute. The terms and conditions of the compounding of the offence will be determined by the Magistrate.

- **Allowance:** A Muslim woman against whom *talaq* has been declared is entitled to seek subsistence allowance from her husband for herself and for her dependent children. The amount of the allowance will be determined by the Magistrate.

- **Custody:** A Muslim woman against whom such *talaq* has been declared is entitled to seek custody of her minor children. The manner of custody will be determined by the Magistrate.

Secular Muslim

Religion is an accident of birth, and I respect every religion while adhering to my faith where no one can be put on par with Allah. I call myself a secular Muslim. Islam treats everyone equally; when we go to the *Kaaba* (the sacred Muslim shrine in Mecca), the beggar and the king stand together as all are equal in the eyes of God.

I am a practicing Muslim and do *namaz* five times a day. *Namaz* teaches discipline and humility, and like yoga, it keeps you fit in body and spirit. My mother raised me this way. I say that I am secular because I am happy to attend *pujas* at friends' homes or have a candle lit at a church on my behalf.

Education is the Key

Whereas Islam is the second largest religion in India, Muslims comprise just about 14 per cent of the population. It is important that they join the mainstream of life, and education plays an important role in achieving this. Modern education is a great tool for empowerment and equality.

Muslims are the second largest populous religious group after Hindus in India but they lag behind when it comes to formal education, which is why their status has collectively suffered.

The Justice Sachar Committee report of 2006 noted that the literacy rate among Muslims is 59.1 per cent while the national average is 64.8 per cent. On 13 August 2020, *The Times of India* reported figures from the National Statistical Office that revealed worrying facts: Seventeen per cent of Muslim youth aged 03–35 had never received formal education, Muslim women were the least educated and that the education of Muslims in general is less than of those belonging to Scheduled Castes and Tribes.

What aggravates the situation is the lack of knowledge about their religion, combined with illiteracy. They believe what they are told without discretion. When you educate a woman, you educate not just a person but her entire family. When a woman prospers, the nation prospers. I am who I am today because of my alma mater, the Sacred Heart Convent in Yercaud, Salem district of Tamil Nadu. The Irish Catholic nuns at the school had a deep and enduring influence on my growing years. They eschewed exclusivity, and all were welcome as human beings.

There was no pressure on us to convert and it didn't matter which faith you came from. They made you feel welcome because their minds were focused on the holistic development of students. The education system at this school opened my horizons and gave me the foundation that has seen me throughout my life. The nuns perhaps shaped my worldview to be of service to those who were on the margins, the have-nots.

I came up against a stone wall when I tried to convince leaders of my own faith to allow me an active role in politics. They were stalwarts in politics and I had hoped for their support. But they could not overcome their patriarchal and bigoted mindset and didn't mentor me or give me a helping hand. I prevailed despite them, not because of them.

Of late, madrasas are going beyond teaching religious texts and adding subjects such as science, IT, maths, and English. This is a positive step but much needs to be done. The recommendations of the Sachar Committee to link madrasas to regular schools as a step towards facilitating mainstreaming of minorities should be implemented.

Burkha & Hijab

Islam is not a regressive religion when it comes to women. Those women who do not wear a *burkha* have every right to make that choice. Clothes are a matter of personal preference and I don't see why wearing or not wearing a *burkha* or a *hijab* is objectionable. Even today, Gujaratis and Marwaris cover their heads as per custom. I do not see anything wrong with this. Instead of focusing on such irrelevant issues, we should focus on the fact that 31 per cent of Muslim women in India are uneducated (*The Times of India*, 13 August 2020), and we should try to ensure they get a good start to life with the right education.

Today, the *hijab* has become very controversial. In Saudi Arabia and the UAE, it is draped more like a fashion accessory with women beautifully made up, wearing tights and a fashionable cloak as a throw over like a *burkha*. They know how to accentuate their features with the right amount of makeup.

In India, the *hijab* is controversial. Every educational institution has their dress code. Some don't accept wearing a *hijab* in classrooms. Once you leave the premises, you're entitled to wear the *hijab*. There are rules to be followed. Muslim girls sitting on *dharna* because they feel they are denied their religious rights are totally wrong. I agree with Firoz Bakht Ahmed, columnist, educator and grandnephew of Maulana Abul Kalam Azad who has said that Muslim girls must follow Islam according to Allah and the Prophet and to educate themselves, and not be influenced by clerics who say otherwise.

I come from a progressive modern family where none of our family members wore the *hijab*—be it my grandmother, mother-in-law or other female members of the family though they were religious and performed their *namaz* five times daily and Haj.

Likewise, both my daughters are strong modern women. I was a hands-on mother and saw to it that they learnt about Islam. We have all performed Haj.

Age of Marriage

I got married at 17 and going by own experience, I feel it is better for girls not to marry at a young age. Young people, irrespective of gender, should study, work, travel, and explore the opportunities available in this vast world and their own potential. All of these might not be possible if they marry at a young age. However, I don't agree that the age of marriage should be increased by law. If you are old enough to vote at 18, you are old enough to marry.

5

Events that Shaped India

IN MY LONG career in politics, I was witness to several critical events that played out at the national level. And while I did not have any role in the decision-making, I was affected by them as a citizen, as a party worker and as a human being. I recollect some key events that had a pivotal impact on the country. I have tried to be objective in my assessment.

Indira & The Emergency

Mrs Indira Gandhi was my role model from the age of 13. While other teenagers had film stars and musicians as their fantasies, it was Indira*ji*'s photo in the newspapers that got me dreaming of politics.

I first saw her in flesh and blood in 1978. She had lost her traditional seat of Rae Bareli in the general elections in 1977 after she lifted the Emergency. Helped by Chief Minister Devaraj Urs, she contested and won the by-election from Chikmagalur (now

Chikkamagaluru) in Karnataka. I met her when she came to thank the voters after winning the Parliament seat from Chikkamagaluru in 1978. What a sight it was to see the victory parade. I can't ever forget that scene; she stood in an open jeep and drove all through the constituency. The number of garlands she got must have run into thousands and she kept throwing them to the public who vied to grab them.

I had driven to Chikkamagaluru from Bengaluru with veteran Congress member Shauqat Qureishi, who had taken me under her wing. We went to the guest house where Indira*ji* was staying. I remember vividly that she patted the couch and asked me to come and sit next to her. I was ecstatic at meeting my hero at long last. It's my eternal regret that I have not been able to get hold of a photograph of that momentous occasion. Yes, she was my hero and I say it unreservedly.

People have questioned me about my views about the Emergency that was imposed in India at the behest of Prime Minister Indira Gandhi from 1975 to 1977. It was triggered by the Allahabad High Court's ruling against her in the case filed by her opponent Raj Narain of the SSP (Samyukta Socialist Party). Indira*ji* had won the general elections in 1971 by a huge margin but Raj Narain, clown though he was, was adamant about getting the seat. He filed a case accusing her of electoral malpractice for misusing government machinery for her campaign. On 12 June 1975, Justice Jagmohanlal Sinha of the Allahabad High Court held that her elections were void, disqualified her from Parliament and imposed a six-year ban on her holding any elected post. Indira*ji* moved the Supreme Court where she was given a conditional stay by the vacation judge. Fearing an adverse ruling when the court resumed, she imposed the Emergency on the pretext of internal disturbance. Most of the vocal Opposition was jailed, the press was censored and several fundamental rights of citizens were suspended.

I don't and I can't deny the several instances of excesses that happened during this period. I had not joined the Congress party at that point of time; I joined it in 1979 when Indira*ji* was not the prime minister. I have also been asked why I decided to join the Congress despite my strong feelings regarding this very controversial period in Indian history.

I will focus on what was, without doubt, one of the most shocking acts – the forced mass sterilisation of people, mostly young men, across the country. Pushed by Sanjay Gandhi, truckloads of unmarried men were carried away to be sterilised. Many of them were from mostly Muslim areas such as Jama Masjid in old Delhi, earning the wrath of the community.

This is something that I found difficult to reconcile myself with, let alone justify. It is estimated that about 8.3 million people were sterilized during the Emergency and that most of these were forced. To understand how this came about, a little bit of background is needed because not many of today's readers would be aware of it.

Genesis of Family Planning

Much has been made in recent years of the 'human capital' of India, and how the youth are fuelling the economic growth of the country. This wasn't always the case; in fact, India's humans were weighing her down and impeding progress.

When the British left India in 1947, they left it much poorer than they found it. After two centuries of colonial rule, 'the brightest jewel in the British Crown was the poorest country in the world in terms of per capita income at the beginning of the 20th century' as former Prime Minister and economist Dr Manmohan Singh observed.

At the time of Independence, India was a poor and over-populated country. With a population of 340 million, its GDP was 2.7 lakh crore, accounting for just 3 per cent of the world's total GDP at that time. More than 50 per cent of India's GDP came from agriculture; it produced about 50 million tonnes of food grains, which was however not enough to feed its people. As much as 90 per cent of the population lived in villages and were dependent mainly on agriculture for subsistence.

Aid was forthcoming from the West and so was an oft-repeated message: 'Control and reduce the rate of birth as your resources can't match your population.' While the rising population had become a matter of concern around the world, the high birth rates in developing countries, combined with increased lifespans that came from better nutrition and healthcare, had set alarm bells ringing.

Prime Minister Jawaharlal Nehru was of the opinion that the problem would be solved if India increased its production by putting to use its population. 'If we increase our production, agricultural and other, [and] if this population is put to work for production, then we are not overpopulated,' he said in 1948, addressing the United Nations Economic Commission for Asia and the Far East (now known as ESCAP). His five-year plans were aimed at creating this balance by increasing agricultural and industrial production.

National Programme

In 1951, Census Commissioner R.A. Gopalaswami, after conducting India's first census post-Independence, was shocked at the results and had pushed for mass sterilisation. He reportedly said that any plan to get more food wouldn't be enough to feed Indians, and suggested that people with three or more children should be sterilised.

His suggestion didn't receive much support due to lack of objective information about vasectomies and thus, the focus in the early years was on trying to get people to use natural methods of birth control such as the rhythm method.

The rhythm method, or the calendar method, works on the system of tracking the menstrual history of a woman to predict when she will ovulate. Avoiding intercourse during a woman's fertile period decreases the risk of pregnancy. Many of us used this method but it was not foolproof and did lead to unwanted pregnancies. (Years later, my husband and I practised it too, and I had to undergo medical termination of pregnancies when the method failed.)

Family planning was part of the Five-Year Plans. In 1952, India was the first country in the world to launch a national programme for family planning. It was intended to reduce the fertility rate and slow birth rate, and ensure that economic growth was not overtaken by a growing population. The government started a series of programmes that ranged from door-to-door campaigns in rural areas to mass media campaigns, and monetary incentives.

'Hum do, hamare do'

Efforts to get Indians to have smaller families in the 1950s and 1960s led to slogans like 'We two, ours two/ *Hum do, hamare do*'. The ideal family picture on the publicity posters depicted a man, a woman, a boy and a girl. It didn't account for the Indian preference for a son, the male heir who would propagate the family line. Not surprisingly, couples who did not bear a son on the first try, tried again, and again and again.

Nandan Nilekani, in his book, *Imagining India: Ideas for the New Century*, cites a court case of a missing daughter. The judge was surprised at her name '*Nirasha*', which means 'disappointment' and asked why the parents had chosen that name. The lawyer replied that it was because she was their fifth daughter!

Contraceptives

The move to different options for birth control was closely linked to food. A year after Nehru's death in 1964, rains failed in India and all the progress that it had made in increasing food cultivation was wiped out. Faced with people on the brink of starvation, Prime Minister Indira*ji* reluctantly turned to the US for help; Nehru had, with similar reluctance, taken food at concessional rates from the US in 1950.

When Indira*ji* visited the US in 1966, President Lyndon Johnson gave her an exceedingly warm welcome and agreed to help India with both money and food at concessional rates. The aid came with strings attached; among the conditions was that India had to make a firmer push to step up population control. President Johnson reportedly said, 'I'm not going to piss away foreign aid in nations where they refuse to deal with their own population problems.' Indira*ji* agreed to increase the country's family planning programmes by offering incentives to people to undergo sterilizations and/or contraceptive measures such as inserting intrauterine devices (IUDs).

Several shiploads of wheat and other food grains arrived from the US, and famine was staved off. After that, India brought about important changes in agriculture that substantially increased food production and security. Indira*ji* actively promoted modern agricultural practices in India from 1968 and adopted the Green Revolution. She endorsed the initiatives of agricultural scientist and plant geneticist Dr M.S. Swaminathan. With high yield varieties of seeds, pesticides and fertilisers, modern irrigation facilities, and equipment such as tractors, there was a substantial increase in the production of food grains, especially wheat and rice.

Population Bomb

In the years that followed, India and Indira*ji* continued to be under great pressure from the West to step up population control programmes. The subject had attracted a lot attention in the West thanks to the publication of a provocatively titled book *The Population Bomb* in 1968. Written by American biologist Paul R. Ehrlich and his wife Anne, the alarmist title was one of two marketing-driven decisions; the second was downright unfair – the publisher dropped Anne's name as the co-author, although she was qualified to be so. In fact, she went on to co-author several books with him.

The book painted a doomsday scenario of global famine in the 1970s and 1980s resulting from overpopulation. It also predicted several other societal upheavals and called for immediate action to curb population growth.

Ehrlich's book begins with a scene in Delhi. 'The streets seemed alive with people… People, people, people, people. As we moved slowly through the mob… the dust, noise, heat, and cooking fires gave the scene a hellish aspect.' No surprise then, that ordinary Americans, philanthropic organisations and politicians alike began to push India and other poor countries to ramp up efforts for contraception and sterilization.

Even while critics pointed out errors in its premise and warned of exaggeration, the book influenced public perception and government policy to a great extent. There was greater urgency in the developed world to curb population growth in developing nations. Plenty of aid was also forthcoming under the stewardship of the UNFPA (UN Population Fund). By the 1970s, Sweden, Norway, The Netherlands and Japan had all increased their aid for India's family planning programme.

Alongside attempts at economic reform to overcome poverty under the catchy slogan of *Garibi Hatao* (remove poverty), family planning became an area of greater priority to deal with the problem of overpopulation for the government. The programmes included sending out trucks around the countryside to dispense condoms and birth control pills, all paid for by rich donor countries.

Some anecdotes are both amusing and depressing, and point out the fallacies of policies that fail to understand the ground reality. Families in villages valued their children; with high rates of infant mortality, each child was an indispensable pair of hands to work the land or do some needed chore. There was also a lack of education and biases that made people reluctant to opt for contraception. In pockets across the country, vasectomies were being carried out and targets had been set. In fact, mass sterilisations had already begun.

The Brash Son

One person who had no patience with the naysayers or his own mother, who he thought was a 'ditherer', was Sanjay Gandhi.

Indira*ji*'s second-born was viewed as her political heir and the *de facto* party boss. In the end, he was 'the son who led his mother astray', as eminent journalist Vinod Mehta described him.

When the Emergency was imposed in June 1975, Sanjay gathered more power and with a large number of young men, set about implementing his pet five-point programme to promote literacy, family planning, tree planting, eradication of casteism and dowry. Undoubtedly, these social ills had and have no place in our society. However, the methods Sanjay and his supporters employed included brute force and complete overriding of individual choice. There was none to oppose him as he rode roughshod over his party and the Opposition leaders had been jailed.

Horrific stories emerged of young, unmarried men being carted away en masse, and it seemed that the poor, and in particular the Muslims, were targeted. Most of the excesses were concentrated in the northern states. Though I was tucked away in Bengaluru, and I hadn't yet joined the Congress, I was shocked and frightened at the accounts that emerged.

Indira*ji* always had the country's best interests at heart in all the policies and programmes. It was in their implementation that things went terribly wrong.

It seemed that Indira*ji* was a victim of her excessive love for her son, and her maternal love had blinded her to his actions and their impact. Perhaps he was the only person she could rely on and that gave him unbridled power. She was not infallible and allowed personal feelings to take priority.

Better sense prevailed and she lifted the Emergency in 1977, reportedly much against the advice of Sanjay.

Following her astounding announcement in January that fresh elections would be held for the Lok Sabha, all top political leaders of the country who were jailed at the beginning of the Emergency got together under the leadership of Jayaprakash Narayan. The Janata Party was born and that set the bells ringing for the diminishing of the clout of the Congress. Indira*ji* lost the next elections and Morarji Desai became the first non-Congress prime minister of the country.

When the Emergency was lifted and the reign of terror ended, I felt it was redemption and my faith in her was strengthened. I was electrified when I finally set eyes on her, at an election rally in Bengaluru in 1979. As for Sanjay, I had met him briefly, just once in Delhi. It was a perfunctory introduction and not long enough for me to even register an impression. Sanjay died after crashing his plane while performing daredevil stunts in Delhi in June 1980. Indira*ji* was completely devastated. As a national leader, however, she had to overcome her pain and pursue her destiny.

Annus Horribilis

The year 1984 was one of the worst years in India's history. In the first week of June, security forces stormed the Harmandir Sahib Complex—the Golden Temple—in Amritsar. Named Operation Blue Star, it was meant to flush out Sikh separatist Jarnail Singh Bhindranwale and supporters of the touted separate Sikh state Khalistan. They had taken over the Akal Takht complex and were accumulating weapons in the holy place of worship for Sikhs. A 72-hour battle ensued between the army and the militants in which over four hundred people were killed, including Bhindranwale, and hundreds more injured. The complex was badly damaged in the battle.

The military action by the state created tensions amongst members of the Sikh community across the world. It also had a terrible and tragic effect a few months later, when Indira*ji* was assassinated by two of her Sikh bodyguards on 31 October 1984. Their motive was revenge against her for giving permission for Operation Blue Star.

I happened to be in New Delhi when Indira*ji* was assassinated. Upon hearing the news, I reeled with shock. I was staying at the Samrat Hotel, and as I stood by the window of my room, I saw smoke billowing into the sky from different parts of the capital. Though I hadn't yet heard the details of what was happening after the news of her assassination spread, I realised that the repercussions of the dastardly crime would be very severe.

I was staying alone at the hotel and was petrified. I rang up Margaret Alva, who was then the All India Mahila Congress president; she was very kind and promptly invited me to come over to her house. I stayed with her that night and the next day I paid my last respects to Indira*ji* at the Teen Murti Bhavan where she lay in state. As I flew back to Bengaluru, leaving behind me a city torn by riots, I wept for the loss of Indira*ji* and the fallout of her tragic death. I grieved at the untimely death of the person who had been such a significant influence in my life.

Indira*ji* had a charisma that was charged with energy and each interaction with her is etched in my memory: my first face-to-face meeting with her at the guest house after her victory parade in Chikkamagaluru, at the Raj Bhavan in Bengaluru when I warned her that Gundu Rao's actions would cost the elections, her kind and encouraging words after my arrest over the custodial death of Munna, and the most memorable meeting at the All India Mahila Convention at the Palace Grounds in September 1984. The traitorous bodyguard Beant Singh who riddled her with bullets a month later was right behind her when I garlanded her then.

The worst fears of the country came true in the hours following Indira*ji*'s assassination. During the anti-Sikh riots that followed, it was reported that nearly 3,000 Sikhs were killed on the streets of Delhi and a few thousands more in different parts of the country. Some Congress leaders were implicated in inciting the pogroms, and after several years, Sajjan Kumar who was an MP at the time of the riots, was sentenced to life imprisonment.

Rajiv Gandhi

Rajiv Gandhi, Indira*ji*'s firstborn, was a pilot with the Indian Airlines. He was a reluctant political heir who entered politics after Sanjay's death in 1980. He was appointed general secretary of the Congress (Indira) in 1983. My first major interaction with him was when he came to Bengaluru to inaugurate the All India Mahila Congress Convention in 1984.

Handsome and rosy-complexioned, Rajiv had a huge following amongst women. I was the head of the City Mahila Congress and was actively helping Margaret with all the preparations. We received him with fanfare and jubilation and the convention was very successful.

From then on, I remember that he was always well-mannered when we met. I had the opportunity to meet him quite often as he used to accompany Margaret and Mani Shankar Aiyar when he visited Karnataka to campaign for the midterm elections. He was a tireless campaigner, and we would be on the road till 2 a.m. at times.

However, in his early years in politics, Rajiv's decisions were sometimes hasty. His inexperience led him to make remarks and take action without thinking of the consequences. Some of them had a long-reaching and detrimental impact on the Congress.

Offending Telugus

In 1982, Rajiv went on a private visit to Hyderabad, and when he alighted at the Begumpet airport, he saw a huge group of people, including an entire band, on the tarmac to receive him. Being a pilot, he probably knew the danger of letting crowds so close to the plane. He was also against showy demonstrations. When the crowd reached him, Rajiv asked who was responsible for bringing them and was told that it was none other than Chief Minister Tanguturi Anjaiah. In a fit of fury, Rajiv lambasted the senior politician, going so far as to calling the chief minister a 'buffoon'.

N.T. Rama Rao, the matinee idol-turned politician, capitalised on the incident, proclaiming it to be an insult to '*Telugu vari atma gauravam* (Telugu pride)'. Rajiv's remark, made in the heat of the moment, was a rallying cry for NTR's Telugu Desam Party (TDP) against the Congress in the 1983 Assembly elections. NTR added salt to the wounds of the Congress by offering five seats to Maneka Gandhi's 'Sanjay Gandhi Vichar Manch'. The TDP won 202 of the 294 seats it contested, and its resounding victory set the stage for the rise of regional parties and the decline of national parties, notably the Congress.

Interestingly, Prime Minister Narendra Modi brought up this incident in Parliament in 2018. It was a crafty bid to neutralise the Telugu Desam, the BJP's coalition partner. The TDP had been upset that the BJP had not kept the promises it had made to the state. Modi adroitly raked up the old issue to show that it was the Congress which had let down the Telugus.

Alienating Lingayats

Rajiv's unexpected actions in removing the chief minister of Karnataka similarly had a major impact in diminishing the party's clout in the state. Chief Minister Veerendra Patil was a strong leader from the Lingayat community, one of the two dominant communities in the state. He had led the Congress to its biggest ever victory in 1989, winning 179 of the 224 seats in the Assembly.

In 1990, Rajiv was the Congress president. Veerendra Patil had suffered a stroke at the beginning of October and soon after, communal riots had broken out in the state as a fallout of the 'Ram rath yatra' taken out by the BJP, the VHP (Vishva Hindu Parishad) and the Sangh Parivar in support of building a temple on the site of the Babri Masjid in Ayodhya. Forty-six people were killed in the riots and the Prime Minister came to visit the affected areas.

Rajiv's first stop was the residence of the bedridden Chief Minister Veerendra Patil. Apparently, Rajiv was shocked to see the seriousness of the stroke's effects—Patil was paralysed and incapacitated. Rajiv felt that in that weak condition, Patil would not be able to give the state the attention it needed during the crisis that still gripped it. After visiting one of the riot-torn areas, he announced at the Bengaluru airport, before flying out of the city, that Karnataka would have a new chief minister in four days.

The drama didn't end there as Patil defiantly refused to quit and also refused to call for a meeting of the Congress Legislature Party to elect a new leader. This led to the imposition of President's Rule in the state, effectively ending Patil's career.

The ramifications ran deeper. The Lingayats, a dominant political community to which Patil belonged, were upset at this insult to a leader from their ranks and dropped their support for the party. Lingayats control the votes in nearly 100 of the 224 Assembly constituencies. The Congress was routed in the 1994 Assembly elections; its seat tally fell from 178 to 34. As *The Hindu* noted:

> The Congress faced a 17% loss of vote share, which was shared predominantly by the BJP and the Janata Dal. BJP's vote share increased from 4% to 16.995% and Janata Dal's from 27.08% to 33.54%. Even though the Janata Dal, which eventually formed the government with the new-found support of Lingayats in 1994, was the immediate beneficiary of this development, the BJP in the subsequent years penetrated deep into the social base of the community.

Since then, the Lingayats have never voted for the Congress en bloc. In a way, B.S. Yediyurappa owes his rise to Rajiv Gandhi; Patil had got Congress the Lingayat votes, and without him, the voters moved to Yediyurappa and the BJP. The alienation of the Lingayats cost the Congress dearly in Karnataka.

Over the years though, Rajiv quickly adapted and learnt to handle politicians in a smoother way.

A BRIEF INTERLUDE

A couple of events transpired that are worthy of being mentioned in my life story. Indira Gandhi did not have a good rapport with her younger daughter-in-law, Maneka. After Sanjay's death, Maneka had assumed that she would get the ticket for the Amethi constituency in Uttar Pradesh, from where Sanjay had won. But Indira*ji* gave it to Rajiv. Maneka formed the Rashtriya Sanjay Manch in 1983.

Gundu Rao and F.M. Khan from Karnataka were staunch Sanjay loyalists and were willing to transfer their devotion to Rajiv. They had gone all out to give him a rousing welcome when he came to attend the national convention of the Youth Congress in Bengaluru in 1982. F.M. Khan, who had a penchant for grand gestures, had organised a float in the shape of a plane for Rajiv to ride into the city from the airport!

But Rajiv did not take to the duo as much as they would have liked him to. And when Maneka formed her party, the Congress high command suspected that they would be joining it. F.M. Khan was expelled in 1984 from the Congress and the party hoped that this would send a signal to Gundu Rao.

After Indira*ji*'s assassination, senior Congress leader and Finance Minister Pranab Mukherjee expected that he would become the prime ministerial candidate. When Rajiv pipped him to the post, a miffed Mukherjee started a new party, the Rashtriya Samajwadi Congress. This was inaugurated in Bengaluru with Gundu Rao and F.M. Khan doing the honours. Gundu Rao sent out feelers to me to join the party. I had absolutely no interest in joining the little upstart party. F.M. Khan, who at that time still had my interests at heart, and knew very well that I wouldn't have much of a future if I left the Congress, brushed off Gundu Rao's invitation to me saying that I wouldn't be bringing anything worthwhile. He must have known that the new party was more noise than substance.

Within a few years, the RSC merged with the Congress after Mukherjee patched up things with Rajiv. Mukherjee then went on to play an important role in India's history. After Rajiv's assassination (on 21 May 1991), P.V. Narasimha Rao became the Prime Minister, and Mukherjee was inducted as a minister. He was given powerful portfolios such as Defence, External Affairs and Finance. With his clout and position in the party unchallenged, Mukherjee steered Sonia Gandhi towards taking charge of the party in 1998. In 2012, Mukherjee was backed by the UPA and became the President of India, a position he held till 2017.

This is an example that shows that in politics one needs brains, guts, determination and luck to succeed.

Youngest PM

When Rajiv Gandhi became the Prime Minister at the age of 40—the youngest PM of the nation to date—he was determined to take India into the 21st century, and quickly. In the five years that he was in power, from 1984 to 1989, he steered a sea change in a variety of sectors that made lives easier for Indians. He appointed experts from outside to the bureaucracy to spearhead these initiatives.

Today, the world acknowledges that India has been able to successfully helm the world's largest vaccination drive against Covid-19. India's vaccine capability was created by the Universal Immunisation Programme powered by Rajiv. The creation of domestic immune production capacity and the establishment of a cold chain for vaccines led to the successful eradication of polio via the Pulse Polio programme. The same infrastructure and knowledge have come in useful for the SARS Covid vaccination drive under way from 2021.

Rajiv can be credited for many steps that bettered the life of Indians and set the foundation of reforms in economy, health, education and human development. He laid the foundation of Panchayati Raj institutions to take democracy to the grassroots level and prepared the ground for the Constitution (73rd and 7th Amendment) Act, 1992 that came into force from 24 April 1993. This enabled villages and towns to become self-governing entities. He also championed the cause of women's reservation by giving 33 per cent of the seats in the Panchayat institutions; this was later increased to 50 per cent.

He empowered Indian youth by reducing the voting age from 21 to 18. This move had a far-reaching impact on the electoral process; 4.7 crore young Indians became eligible to vote for the first time in the elections in 1989 and the figure rose to 8.4 crore first-time voters in 2019.

The anti-defection law introduced in 1985 put an end to the frequent defections and horse-trading that was prevalent in political parties—a practice that was infamously dubbed as '*Aaya Ram, Gaya Ram*' (a joking term for turncoats who switch political parties frequently).

Science, Technology and Telecom witnessed remarkable progress during Rajiv's regime. As Sam Pitroda, who as an adviser to Rajiv, laid the foundation of India's telecom and technology revolution in the 1980s, wrote in *The Week*:

> Rajiv was a gift to India at the right time because he was young, open, and with fresh views on politics, development and society. He gave rise to hope. He had the vision to take India into the 21st century with new ideas, dignity and compassion. India is now a nation of a connected billion. We have software service exports worth

$200 billion. The seeds for this were planted in the Rajiv era...Rajiv was willing to explore new frontiers and was ready to support new thought.

In a country that barely had even one per cent telephone coverage, Rajiv was responsible for connecting 90 per cent of India through PCOs (public call offices). He ushered in an era of computerisation in government offices. The reduction of import quotas, taxes and tariffs on technology-based industries led to the creation of home-grown IT companies, many of which have become global leaders today and set India on the map as a digital powerhouse.

When the US refused to allow technology transfer to India for a supercomputer for weather forecasting fearing it would be used for defence purposes instead, Rajiv set up the C-DAC (Centre for Development of Advanced Computing). This Centre created India's first indigenous supercomputer, the PARAM 8000. Rajiv also stood up to the US when it tried to pressurise him to stop the testing of the Agni ballistic missile in 1989. He hailed the successful launch of the missile as a step toward safeguarding India's independence. He claimed there was 'a great deal of misinformation being spread by and in interested quarters about this technology'. He stated that while India had no interest in nuclear weapons, the country lost its independence two centuries ago because of a lack of vigilance. 'We must remember that technological backwardness also leads to subjugation.... Never again will we allow our freedom to be so subjugated,' the PM said.

He worked for peace within the country, arriving at accords in Punjab, Assam and Mizoram. The Rajiv-Longowal Accord or the Punjab Accord in 1985 helped bring normalcy to Punjab. The accord with the All Assam Students Union, also in 1985, put an end to six years of strife in the north eastern state and brought the largest student union into the mainstream of life. In 1986, he signed a peace agreement with Mizo insurgent leader Laldenga and granted statehood to Mizoram.

He created a more positive atmosphere with neighbours like China (he was the first Prime Minister to visit China after a gap of 34 years in December 1988) and in the subcontinent, with Pakistan, Bangladesh, and Sri Lanka. However, as Prime Minister, Rajiv Gandhi also took some decisions that were unwelcome and had a backlash.

Shah Bano Case

In April 1978, Shah Bano, a 62-year-old Muslim woman, filed a petition in court demanding maintenance for herself and her five children from her husband Mohammed Ahmad Khan, a lawyer, who had divorced her. Khan claimed that he need not pay maintenance under the Muslim Personal Law in India. The All India Muslim Personal Law Board supported Khan and said that the courts could not interfere in matters that are under Muslim Personal Law.

The High Court granted Shah Bano's right to maintenance under Section 125 of the Code of Criminal Procedure, 1973, and the Supreme Court upheld the verdict and increased the maintenance due to her. The SC also ruled that the CrPC applies to all Indian citizens regardless of their religion.

While the verdict was welcomed by Muslim women and by sections who wanted a Uniform Civil Code, the Congress under Rajiv Gandhi did a volte-face. In a bid to appease fundamentalist Muslim men and the self-appointed *maulvis*, the government used its majority in the Lok Sabha to push through the Muslim Women (Protection of Rights on Divorce) Act, 1986. This law effectively overturned the Supreme Court verdict in the Shah Bano case by saying that a man had to pay his divorced wife and their children maintenance only during the *iddat* period, which is usually three months after the divorce.

The Act was a regressive and ill-conceived move by the government and was widely criticised for damaging the dignity and safety of women. I was opposed to the Act and could not agree with the reactionary Muslim men and women in the Congress like Mohsina Kidwai and Najma Heptulla who supported the Sharia against women like Shah Bano. It's sad that these privileged women had no sympathy for the hardships of their poorer sisters.

Anti-Defamation Bill

Rajiv Gandhi's government ran into rough weather in 1988 for trying to enact what is known as 'one of the most draconian bills' in India. The Defamation Bill sought to place the burden of proof on the accused in defamation suits. It gave ample scope for any politician or bureaucrat who disliked what was reported about them to file a case against a journalist. Incensed by this bid to muzzle them, the entire media of the country joined hands in protest. Faced with such severe opposition from the media, lawyers, students and several Congress members themselves, the Prime Minister was forced to withdraw it.

Bofors Scandal

On the icy slopes 8,000 ft above sea level, India fought the Kargil War against Pakistan in 1999. Many brave soldiers played heroic roles. One of the heroes who won the war for India was the Bofors Howitzer gun. As *India Today* described it, 'Bofors, with a range of over 35 km in the high-altitude terrain, proved to be the difference between the two armies in Kargil. Bofors could fire three rounds in 12 seconds. Its ability to target enemy posts at close to 90-degree angles made it operate literally from under the nose of Pakistani soldiers who were occupying the hilltops.' But 10 years earlier, a corruption scandal over the procurement of these guns cost Rajiv Gandhi, and the Congress, the 1989 general elections.

The allegations of corruption began with a news report on a Swedish radio station on 16 April 1987. It said that the US$1.3 billion (Rs 1,437 crore) contract that the Swedish arms manufacturer Bofors had signed with India in 1986 included a 3 per cent commission to middlemen and agents. It was alleged that top Indian politicians and defence personnel were involved in securing the contract to purchase 400 howitzers. Most of the US$40 million bribe was reported to have been paid into Swiss bank accounts in May 1986. It was alleged that the Swedish company paid nearly Rs 64 crore as bribe to politicians, Congress leaders and bureaucrats.

Rajiv had announced that his politics would not be old-school and among the many campaigns he launched was a war against corruption. He used the occasion of the centenary of the Congress at the AICC session in Mumbai in December 1985 to spell out his stance and he was given the epithet 'Mr Clean'. He denied any wrongdoing in the arms deal and asked the Swedish government to investigate it. But it blew up into one of the biggest corruption scandals in the world. The Opposition seized upon it. Defence Minister V.P. Singh resigned from the ministry and the next year formed the Janata Dal with various other factions of the Janata Party. He led the Opposition's election battle against the Congress on the corruption issue.

'*Gali gali mein shor hai, Rajiv Gandhi chor hai* (The word on the streets is that Rajiv Gandhi is a thief)' caught on and the Congress lost the general elections in November 1989. My friend Mani Shankar Aiyar, who was Rajiv Gandhi's aide, told me that when they started the campaign from Mathura, the crowd that attended the election rally was very sparse. Mani said, 'The writing on the wall was very clear that it was a losing battle,' and sure enough, his fears came true. V.P. Singh became the Prime Minister of the National Front government with the support of the BJP and Left. (Rajiv is supposed to have termed it a 'National Affront').

The Bofors case and the CBI (Central Bureau of Investigation) probe into it went on for several years with many eye-popping revelations. But none of the allegations were proved.

In March 2011, the CBI was allowed by the court to withdraw the case against Italian businessman Ottavio Quattrocchi, the alleged middleman in the deal.

Here, I would like to quote Dr R.K. Raghavan, former CBI chief, who investigated the Bofors deal.

> Many persons, in and out of government, have, over time, asked me whether there was evidence of any payment made directly to Rajiv. My emphatic response has remained the same: there was not the slightest evidence to this effect. The big question mark was, and is, with regard to the money received by Quattrocchi and the Hindujas, both known for links with the Gandhi family. It is possible some of the payments were meant for the Congress party. It is difficult, however, to confirm this.

Out of office, Rajiv worked ceaselessly to boost the Congress. When V.P. Singh's government collapsed in less than a year, the

Congress supported Chandra Shekhar's splinter group of the Janata Dal in forming a minority government. Four months later, the Congress withdrew its support and the government fell in March 1991. Fresh general elections were scheduled in May-June the same year.

Rajiv toured the whole country on a mission to bring the Congress back to power with a full majority in the Lok Sabha. When he came to Karnataka, I saw with my own eyes that his fingers were swollen and bleeding as a result of shaking hands with the public. He had ceaseless energy and loved to move amongst the people, charming them with his charismatic smile and friendliness.

It was during one such meeting on 21 May 1991 at an election rally at Sriperumbudur in Tamil Nadu that he was blown to smithereens by a suicide bomber belonging to the Liberation Tigers of Tamil Eelam (LTTE). The 'live' bomb was Dhanu, a young woman who came up on the pretext of garlanding him. Along with Rajiv, 14 others were killed in the bomb explosion. The assassination was in retaliation for his actions in sending the Indian Peace Keeping Force (IPKF) to Sri Lanka during its civil war. The most promising PM, the one we had pinned our hopes on, had lost his life in a tragic replay of his mother's death. He never lived to see the day of bringing the Congress back to power. It was such a tragic end to a kind and charming visionary.

When Rajiv was assassinated, I was in Delhi on party work. I can never forget the sight that I witnessed when I went to pay my last respects to the departed soul. Everyone there – man, woman, child – was weeping. But Sonia*ji* stood in dignified silence; her grief was covered by the pair of dark glasses on her face, while her children, Rahul and Priyanka, stood on either side. She was like a statue made of stone, her unexpressed grief palpable in her silence.

Strong & Silent PM

P.V. Narasimha Rao's case is a classic example of the saying, 'some have greatness thrust upon them'. Rajiv was assassinated between the first and second phases of the elections. No party won a majority but the Congress could cobble together a minority government. The Maratha strongman Sharad Pawar claimed his stake to become PM, as did N.D. Tiwari from Uttar Pradesh and Arjun Singh from Madhya Pradesh. The quiet and scholarly Narasimha Rao from the southern state of Andhra Pradesh was chosen over the other three. He had been Union Minister for External Affairs, Defence, Home and Human Resources Development in the cabinets of Indira Gandhi and Rajiv Gandhi, had been the Chief Minister of Andhra and the general secretary of the Congress. His credentials were excellent.

Power can be the elixir of youth and it certainly was the case for this accidental prime minister. This veteran from the south had announced his retirement from politics. But fate willed otherwise and he became Prime Minister a week before his 70th birthday, in June 1991.

He seldom spoke but his actions turned India completely around. I can proudly say that Narasimha Rao's tenure as PM from 1991 to 1996 was a golden period for the country. The infamous licence-control *Permit Raj* that had held industry to ransom was given a speedy farewell. He chose Dr Manmohan Singh, who was an economist and not a politician, as his finance minister. The two steered the liberalisation of the Indian economy and set it on the course of modernisation through many structural reforms. The economic and foreign policy initiatives taken during his tenure impacted India's swift rise as a global economic and political power.

Babri Masjid Demolition

Although Narasimha Rao was the first Congress prime minister from outside the Nehru family to successfully complete the full tenure of five years, from 1991-1996, his tenure is indelibly tarnished by the demolition of the Babri Masjid. This 16th century mosque in Ayodhya, Uttar Pradesh, was claimed by right wing Hindus as the Ram Janmabhoomi; they said that a temple had been replaced by a mosque by the Mughals and they wanted this historical wrong corrected.

Efforts to reinstate it as a temple had been going on at various levels from the 1850s and picked up momentum in the 1980s. It became a political issue under the leadership of the VHP and allied groups. A district court ordered in 1986 that Hindus could pray at the monument. Rajiv Gandhi's government backed this decision and allowed *shilanyas* (ground breaking ceremony for temple) to be performed.

In September 1990, BJP leader L.K. Advani backed by the VHP, the RSS (Rashtriya Swayamsevak Sangh), and the BJP, led thousands of *kar sevaks* (religious volunteers) in a campaign to build the Ram Temple at the site. Bloody skirmishes followed and matters kept escalating.

On 6 December 1992, it is estimated that there were over 150,000 people at a rally addressed by Advani, Murli Manohar Joshi and Uma Bharti. One young man carrying a saffron flag managed to climb on top of the mosque and triggered a mob attack on the building. In a matter of hours, the mosque was brought down.

The entire nation watched the action play out on television. I was in the house of Union Minister Salman Khurshid and a group of us watched the demolition of the masjid on BBC. We were aghast; neither Salman nor any of the other senior Muslim ministers—Ghulam Nabi Azad or Jaffer Sharief—could get through to the PM, to ask him to stop it. The incident led to communal clashes across the country, with at least 2,000 people being killed.

Till today, nobody knows why the PM did not act; he certainly never gave an explanation. Perhaps if all the Muslim ministers in the Congress had resigned, he might have stopped the demolition. While Uttar Pradesh was ruled by the BJP at the time, the demolition cost the Congress the support of the Muslims, not only in Uttar Pradesh but across India. It also ripped apart the facade of India's secular fabric. Secular Indians, not just Muslims, felt betrayed by the Prime Minister and the Congress.

For Muslims like me in the Congress, it was a double whammy as we had no answers to give when people questioned about the demolition. The Muslim vote bank castigated us for stabbing them in the back. They said, '*BJP is a khula dushman* (known enemy), *but Congress is a chupa hua dushman* (a hidden enemy).' All I could say was that I agreed with them. Like most liberals, I felt that the Babri Masjid should have been declared as a national monument.

Rao's inaction was seen as being complicit in the act and the Congress paid a heavy price for it. In the 1994 legislative elections in Karnataka, the Congress came a miserable third, winning just 34 seats, and across India, the party was routed in the general elections in 1996.

The contentious matter of the Ayodhya dispute was finally resolved by the Supreme Court on 9 November 2019. It ordered that the disputed land comprising 2.77 acres should be handed over to a trust to be created by the Central government to build the Ram temple. The court ordered the government to give five acres of land in another place to the Uttar Pradesh Sunni Central Waqf Board to build a mosque.

Back in 1996, though Advani*ji*'s Rath Yatra across the country popularized Hindutva, the BJP did not win an overwhelming majority. Atal Bihari Vajpayee*ji* formed a government but had to step down in less than two weeks. In a completely unexpected turn of events, the United Front chose the Vokkaliga strongman from my own state Karnataka, former Chief Minister H.D. Deve Gowda of the Janata Dal, as the consensus candidate for PM. Such is the way destiny works! In a year's time, Deve Gowda and Congress president Sitaram Kesri had a falling out. The Prime Minister invited S.M. Krishna and Dhawan for breakfast to seek their support in stopping the Congress from withdrawing support to his government. I discussed the matter with Gowda on the phone and assured him that he had nothing to worry and that they would succeed. While they were having breakfast, Kesri went to the President of India and gave a letter withdrawing the Congress support to Gowda's government! Gowda was replaced as Prime Minister by I.K. Gujral, but the Congress withdrew its support in November 1997.

The political instability led to general elections being called three years earlier than scheduled, and in 1998, once again there was a hung Parliament. Yet again, Vajpayee formed the government consisting of the National Democratic Alliance (NDA, a big tent alliance of the right-wing BJP and the Shiv Sena, and a few regional parties). A year later, the AIADMK withdrew its support and yet again general elections were called for in 1999. This time, the NDA had the support of many more parties and won with a full majority.

Vajpayee served as the Prime Minister for a full term of five years. However, despite the government's attempts to showcase 'India Shining', the NDA lost the next general elections in 2004. The Congress came back to power, helming the United Progressive Alliance (UPA, a big tent alliance consisting of various Centre-Left parties).

Manmohan Singh, Rao's Finance Minister and later the Leader of the Opposition, became the Prime Minister. He spoke even less than Narasimha Rao had done, if that were possible. He was mocked for being 'Maun Mohan Singh' and for being Sonia*ji*'s puppet. Undaunted by criticism, he quietly went about creating sweeping changes in the economy. The economist PM steered the country's economic growth; in 2007, India achieved its highest GDP growth rate of 9 per cent and became the second fastest-growing major economy in the world.

He reformed the banking and financial sectors, and introduced pro-industry policies such as the VAT and Special Economic Zones (SEZ); he also helped relieve farmers' debts. His government enacted the National Rural Employment Guarantee Act (NREGA) in 2005. This social security scheme provides income security to rural families by providing a minimum of 100 days of definite wage employment in one year.

Manmohan Singh continued into a second term, winning the 2009 elections. He created history by becoming only the second PM after Nehru to complete a full second term in office.

But in 2014, the Congress's chances were marred by reports of corruption and scandals that tarnished the UPA-2. 'Nine years, nine scams', as *India Today* reported. Neither Sonia nor Manmohan Singh could stop the rot that had set in. This was one of the factors that led to the rout of the UPA-2. The more important factor though was that India had gone through a powerful change: right-wing politics had made an impact beyond their traditional bastions and had pervaded all across India. Going beyond the North and the West, the BJP had firmly established itself in the South, the East and the North East.

As Abheek Barman commented in *The Economic Times*,

> The BJP was expected to do well in Delhi, Rajasthan, Madhya Pradesh and Chhattisgarh, where it faced the Congress head-on and where it did well in recent assembly polls. But it has also scooped up seats in states like Uttar Pradesh and Bihar, breaking through old barriers of caste.... This breakdown of caste barriers, to create a consolidated Hindu vote bank across large swathes of India, is probably the greatest achievement of the Modi campaign.

The UPA's electoral battle led by Rahul Gandhi proved to be disastrous. The Congress and the UPA slumped in numbers, being unable to muster even 59 seats, the requisite number to be treated as the main Opposition in the Lok Sabha. It won only 44 seats while it had won 206 seats in the 2009 general election. The BJP won enough votes to form the government on its own had it wanted to.

A triumphant Narendra Modi, the former Chief Minister of Gujarat, who had been projected as the NDA's prime ministerial candidate, became the Prime Minister in 2014. He grew from strength to strength and the BJP increased its votes in the 2019 elections, sweeping the NDA back to power. The Congress failed to get 10 per cent of the seats to earn the post of the Leader of the Opposition.

Hope for India

The BJP has an overwhelming majority of seats in the Parliament and state Assemblies which makes me wonder if the world's largest democracy has devolved into a single-party system. Sonia should invite the splinter groups of the Congress, such as the NCP, TNA, TRS, NCP and Trinamool Congress, to come together. It's vital to build a strong Opposition to ensure a healthy democracy.

I hope that religion does not continue to become a bigger divisive issue and that leaders from across political divides can work together. When I became an MLC in 1994 and a minister in 1999, at times it seemed that my BJP colleagues were more supportive of me than my own party members and colleagues. Even the stalwarts of the BJP treated me with respect. While I was the Minister of Science and Technology in Karnataka, Murli Manohar Joshi was the Union Minister of Science and Technology. I used to interact a lot with him and I found him to be very helpful. He gave me an additional budget from the Centre for a Science Park. I also used to meet Advani*ji* in the Central Hall, and he as well as Joshi*ji* were courteous.

6

Indira to Rahul: The Big Slide

WHAT A TURN of events for the Grand Old Party! Now that I am not involved in active politics and am a social worker, I have nothing to lose and will speak the truth out loud about the prospects, or lack of them, of the Congress.

The Congress failed to acknowledge the growing might of the right-wing parties. Rahul Gandhi's leadership has been disastrous; as the vice-president of the Congress, he led the campaign in the 2014 general elections and the Congress won just 44 seats. In 2019, he led the campaign as the president of the party and the Congress won 52 seats. Rahul even lost his family constituency Amethi in Uttar Pradesh to Smriti Irani of the BJP and became an MP only because he had also contested from Wayanad, Kerala.

Rahul does speak about important topics and has valid points, but they go over the common man's head. Instead of talking about Rafale, he should be talking about what people are concerned about, that is, *roti, kapda aur makaan* (food, clothing and shelter). When he was the Congress vice-president in 2013, Rahul embarrassed Prime Minister Manmohan Singh by saying that the government's ordinance shielding convicted MPs was 'nonsense' and 'should be torn up and thrown away'. Rahul's stand was correct but the way he denounced his own government's action publicly was astounding. He does not seem to have learned from experience, and the BJP makes fun of him as *pappu* and *lallu* (foolish).

He resigned as the party president after the 2019 defeat and Sonia took over again as the party president despite her failing health. If Sonia was not so obsessed with Rahul *baba*, she could do a much better job as the party president. But there is no place for any other leader to grow in the Congress. I'm only telling the truth, blunt as it might sound. The way the party has been run is shocking. Political pundits have commented extensively on the existential crisis that has beset the Congress. The more pertinent question is how is it handling the crisis and is there a concrete plan to overcome it? Judging by the action, rather, the lack of action, it seems to be clutching at straws.

The ongoing Covid-19 crisis and the grave problems of inflation and unemployment offer a great opportunity to take on the government but the Congress has not initiated a coherent attack which could rally the Opposition together. Rather, the party high command is preoccupied with protecting its own turf. Rahul won't move out and make way for anyone else. His sister Priyanka Vadra doesn't seem inclined to take on a bigger or direct role.

Group of 23

In August 2020, a group of 23 senior leaders—members of the Congress Working Committee (CWC), MPs, former Union ministers and former chief ministers—wrote to Sonia seeking reforms in the party's functioning. They sought 'visible and available leadership, organisational restructure and ideological rejuvenation of the party'. They included Ghulam Nabi Azad, Anand Sharma, Bhupinder Singh Hooda, Kapil Sibal, Mukul Wasnik, Shashi Tharoor and Manish Tewari. Expectedly, the CWC crushed the nascent challenge, with Rahul calling it an 'insult' to his mother.

A year later, when Kapil Sibal remarked that 'G-23 is no *Ji Huzoor* 23' and he would continue to raise questions, Youth Congress workers attacked his house. The high command did nothing to stop them nor did it criticise such attacks. This sends a clear message that there can never be democracy within the Congress. Sibal quit the Congress in May 2022 and was elected to the Rajya Sabha as an independent candidate from Uttar Pradesh with the support of the Samajwadi Party in July.

During Rajiv Gandhi's time, Ghulam Nabi Azad gave up his post as a Union Minister and worked to build the Congress party. As AICC general secretary, he masterminded the 'Panchajanya yatra' in Karnataka in 1999. In order to demonstrate unity amongst the bickering factions, he came up with the plan for state party president S.M. Krishna to lead all the Congress MLAs and MLCs in several busloads on a tour across the state. This is just one example of Ghulam Nabi's brilliant work for the Congress; there are countless over the years. It's sad that he was criticised for accepting India's third highest civilian award, the Padma Bhushan. The carping by Congress spokespersons reeks of pettiness and is distasteful. He too quit the Congress in August 2022, sadly noting that he was 'forced to leave home' (meaning that the Congress had been his home). He is among several senior Congress leaders who quit the party, including Kapil Sibal, Jitin Prasada, Yoganand Shastri, Ashwani Kumar, R.P.N. Singh and Sunil Jakhar.

Drama in Karnataka

In my state of Karnataka, the Congress was in power from 2013 to 2018. However, it did not win the majority in the subsequent elections. Though it was a hung Assembly, the BJP's scam-tainted Yediyurappa managed to form the government. He fell short of the majority by seven votes, but was still sworn in as CM by Governor Vajubhai Vala. However, he could not muster a majority, thanks to the Congress strongman D.K. Shivakumar's efforts. Many shenanigans ensued with Yediyurappa having to resign and H.D. Kumaraswamy (Deve Gowda's son) becoming the CM under the Cong-JD(S) combine in May 2018. Kumaraswamy was Chief Minister earlier, from 2006 to 2007 as part of a JD(S)-BJP government and there had been a lot of agreements and disagreements between the BJP's Yediyurappa and him about handing over the chief ministership.

Even the second term of Kumaraswamy's government lasted just 14 months. In the infamous strategy dubbed 'Operation Kamala 2.0' (to engineer defections), 17 MLAs were lured by the BJP, resigned and fled the city. Though the Speaker disqualified them, these MLAs got relief from the Supreme Court. It upheld their disqualification but allowed them to stand for re-election in the by-polls in December 2019; a majority of them won and were reinstated as ministers with plum portfolios in the new Yediyurappa government.

Dogged efforts by Yediyurappa helped him become CM for the fourth term. This was the first time that somebody became the chief minister of the state for the fourth time. In July 2021, prodded by growing dissent amongst party leaders in the state, the BJP top brass forced Yediyurappa to quit. He was replaced by Home Minister Basavaraj Bommai (whose father S.R. Bommai was the Chief Minister in 1988).

These developments have not brightened the prospects of the Congress in Karnataka though. We have an ocean of talent in Karnataka but I don't know if the younger lot in the party will ever get a chance. I feel very sorry for the youngsters in the party like D.K. Shivakumar, Dinesh Gundu Rao, Prakash Rathod, Krishna Byre Gowda and others who have a lot of potential and have been loyal and committed party members. They will win their seats but will the party come to power again here? The rivalry between senior leaders and the internal conflicts are detrimental to the party.

None of us could have imagined that the Congress would be reduced to these circumstances. Everyone had thought that the Congress was like an ocean which would never dry up; it has now been reduced to a minority. The BJP-led NDA currently controls the government of India as well as the government of 18 Indian states, and three Union Territories. The Congress controls three states and has just 53 MPs. There are two people who run the Congress and supposedly the Opposition, Sonia and Rahul. The mother and son combine have rendered both the party and the Opposition effete.

My Political Epitaph

Here's the epitaph of my political life: It began with Indira Gandhi, and it ended with her grandson Rahul Gandhi.

I admire Rahul for the actions he has taken to reduce corruption within the party; at one point, a famous leader had remarked that the symbol of the Congress should be changed from a hand to a hand with a briefcase. Rahul changed all this by firmly refusing to allow seats to be given to the highest bidder. But he treated me harshly without cause. Let me tell you how he behaved with me, a long-time loyal Congress member and former minister. Though a reluctant politician, Rahul Gandhi wields considerable influence on party affairs, even before and after his stint as the party president. (He was the AICC president from 16 December 2017 to 10 August 2019.)

In 2016, a few of us from Karnataka had gone to meet him with various requests; somebody wanted to continue as the chairperson of a Board, and somebody else wanted him to put in a word for some other post. I wanted to be re-nominated to the Legislative Council under the category of social worker and I gave my application to Rahul. It is the norm for leaders to take the applications with a polite, 'I'll look into it.'

Rahul, however, opened my application immediately. He saw a doctor's picture on my brochure and questioned me about it. 'What is he doing here?' he asked curtly. I told him that he was a renowned heart surgeon and I had worked closely with him for several years to help underprivileged people. He told me bluntly, 'Because of him you are disqualified.' He told me, 'I will never entertain you again and I will never give you an appointment.' There were 22 leaders from Karnataka present in the room. Rahul rejected me in front of all of them and nobody said anything in my defence. The news spread and my detractors were elated at my humiliation.

Rahul's treatment of me was in complete contrast to my experience with his father years ago. I had managed to get a meeting with Rajiv to ask him to make me an MLC, and when I began to speak, tears flowed from my eyes as I was overcome by emotion. I was hurting because I had been pursuing my political dream for 14 years to no avail. I would go to Delhi every two years, pleading for my seat. 'Ram's *vanvas* ended after 14 years, when will I come out of the wilderness?' I asked Rajiv. He was sympathetic and courteous. He offered a tissue from the box on his table and said, 'Here, dry your tears, don't cry.'

Rahul's public humiliation of me made me furious. I was further upset with the Congress about its reluctance to take a stand on the Muslim Personal Law concerning triple *talaq*. [I have elaborated my views on the topic in the chapter on Gender & Religion @ Work. Ultimately, when the Muslim Women (Protection of Rights on Marriage) Bill, 2017 came up for a vote in 2019, the Congress also voted in its favour with some caveats.]

I decided to quit the party, as I felt that the way things were going in the Congress, there was no party to speak of. I resigned from the primary membership of the Congress in 2017. In my brief letter to Sonia Gandhi, I mentioned my long membership of the party from 1978. I thanked her for having made me a minister, the first Muslim woman to become one; I expressed my pain at being ignored in my own state while the party's central leaders did not have time for me. My letter was not acknowledged. After all the years and many interactions, my pain did not even merit a response. Things had changed a lot since the early days when I interacted freely with Sonia.

I first set eyes on Sonia at F.M. Khan's house in Delhi. When F.M. Khan was an MP, he kindly invited me, a political novice then, to his house when Indira and Sonia came to see his garden. F.M. Khan had a house on Teen Murti Road; he had amazingly green fingers and his garden used to win awards regularly. The garden that day was a sight for the Gods but I was stunned by Sonia, an auburn-haired beauty in a long skirt.

Over the years, my admiration for Sonia grew; I think she has become more Indian than any of us. It's not just because she wears saris or speaks Hindi; I believe that she has become an Indian in her mind. She educated herself about the caste system in India and the caste dynamics in each state. I remember when S.M. Krishna wanted to be the KPCC president, she sent Dhawan to meet him and check if he had the support of the Vokkaliga mutts (Vokkaligas are a dominant community in Karnataka; mutts are religious organisations whose leaders have great influence over voters and are hence wooed by politicians). She was aghast when D.K. Shivakumar and I lobbied for S.M. Krishna to be made party president of Karnataka. She considered him a white-collared politician who was not in touch with rural voters.

When Sonia contested in Bellary in 1999, I worked with Ambika Soni and supervised the campaigning. We requested Sonia to leave behind her daughter Priyanka to continue the campaign but Priyanka refused to stay back.

We had quite a few interactions after Sonia became the party president and I became a minister. She has always been warm to me. When my enemies complained to her about me and gave her a dossier that claimed that I had been drinking and dancing at a party, she told me, 'I am not an old hag but in public life, you have to maintain a certain decorum.'

Sonia would have one-to-one meetings and would not have a third person around when we spoke. She certainly knows about Indian culture and heritage and I was pleasantly surprised when she once rightly identified that my blouse had *Toda* embroidery (done by the Toda tribals of the Nilgiris, in Tamil Nadu). It's nice to share a feminine bond sometimes.

On a visit to Bengaluru, she was staying at the Raj Bhavan. She had a hectic programme in Mysuru the following day. She was invited by the Suttur Swamiji of the JSS (Jagadguru Sri Shivarathreeshwara muth) to show the philanthropic work that the organisation was doing in feeding and educating thousands of children. B. Janardhana Poojary, the party president and S.M. Krishna, the Chief Minister, were in a meeting with her. I waited with other ministers outside. Much to my surprise, an officer from the SPG (Special Protection Group) came to me and said that Madam had summoned me. I was taken aback and wondered if I had done something wrong.

I was ushered into her room where she politely asked me to take a seat. She was holding a pamphlet that showed the Suttur Swamiji with Murali Manohar Joshi, the BJP stalwart. She asked me if Swamiji was inclined towards the BJP and if she should cancel her scheduled trip to Mysuru. I assured her that the muth was philanthropic and had nothing to do with the BJP. I felt honoured that she had sought my opinion, amongst all the ministers present. We proceeded to Mysuru as planned; en route, we stopped for breakfast at the muth. I was amused to see the way she absolutely relished the *dosa*s that we were served. Back in Bengaluru that evening, she attended an event at the Indian Institute of Science and by virtue of being Science & Technology Minister, I was elated to be given the role of minister-in-waiting.

One action of Sonia's did not sit well with me though. After the demise of former Prime Minister Narasimha Rao in December 2004, the Congress did not treat his body with the respect he deserved. At the behest of Sonia, his body was not even allowed into the AICC building though he was a steadfast Congress member. Nor was he cremated in Delhi with the honour due to a former Prime Minister. Senior Congress functionaries moved his body to Hyderabad, much against the wishes of his family. Sonia didn't trust Rao at all and perhaps this was the reason for the shoddy treatment meted out to him. This was not the way to treat the person who in my opinion was the best Prime Minister of India.

After Sonia and Rahul, Ahmad Patel *bhai* was the most powerful man in the Congress dispensation. Right through Sonia's tenure as chairperson of UPA-1 and 2, he remained her political secretary. If we went to meet Sonia about matters concerning our states, she would tell us to go to Ahmad *bhai* and get vetted. Unfortunately, he had no time to hear the second rung leaders as he was always busy with meetings with *mullahs*. It was a Herculean effort to get an appointment with him. The only way I got to see him was by gate-crashing when a few VIP cars entered his premises. At times, I was treated badly by his watchman who would slam the gate on my face and chase me away like a pariah. He had time to sit down with the *mullahs* and *maulvis* from his home state Gujarat. Perhaps he didn't like me because I was a Muslim woman.

Once I had given a cheque of Rs 2 lakh for party funds. After six months, the cheque was returned to me. I found it very humiliating and felt insulted. Ahmad *bhai* was not warm like Ghulam Nabi Azad. Perhaps he was busy collecting party funds from the Middle East and was indispensable.

I used to attend all the AICC sessions, and I was there in Kolkata when Sonia joined the party in December 1997. I was also there in Delhi when she took over as the party president from Sitaram Kesri in March 1998. Sonia conducts herself well and she is authoritative. Like most Italian mothers who are known for their overriding affection for their sons, Sonia's only weakness is her son.

Coming back to my resignation, I was hurt that Sonia had turned a deaf ear. She didn't even ask any of the national leaders within the party to respond to me. Senior political journalist Naheed Ataulla reported in the *Times of India* about my decision to quit:

> The triple *talaq* issue, which reportedly swung Muslim women's votes in favour of the BJP in Uttar Pradesh, found resonance in Karnataka as former minister Nafees Fazal resigned from the Congress on Tuesday and is all set to join the BJP.
>
> She was upset that the Congress had not taken a stand on the instant triple *talaq* controversy and AICC vice-president Rahul Gandhi reportedly humiliated her when she went to seek a ticket. In her resignation letter to Congress president Sonia Gandhi, she said: 'The reasons are best known to you. I was unable to get an appointment to meet and share my grievances with you. From then onwards, I was humiliated by the state Muslim leaders as our chief minister, Siddaramaiah being new to the party, gave them a free hand.'
>
> Fazal is exploring the option of joining the BJP considering she has a good rapport with former Union Minister S.M. Krishna who recently joined the saffron party. She was a minister in Krishna's government. Fazal is the second person to raise the banner of revolt against the Congress; on Monday, senior party man M.V. Rajasekharan praised Prime Minister Narendra Modi's policies. 'Rahul is too immature to lead the party,' she said.
>
> Fazal, who started her political career with former Prime Minister Indira Gandhi in 1978, said she had plans to join the BJP a decade ago when D.V. Sadananda Gowda was the party president. 'I have suffered in the Congress for 10 years,' she added.

I announced that I was thinking of joining the BJP. I was genuinely impressed by Modi's decision over the triple *talaq* issue and felt that perhaps I could indeed work with the BJP in creating a broader consensus and help overcome the communal elements.

My beloved leader, S.M. Krishna, had quit the Congress and moved to the BJP a few days earlier, and I thought that if he saw merit in that party, I could perhaps find a place for myself there. Yediyurappa, the BJP stalwart in Karnataka, blocked my entry as I was a fiery Muslim woman who had confronted him earlier over the Telgi stamp paper case.

Over time, however, I realised that communal roots were far too deeply entrenched in the BJP. A couple of years later, it dawned on me that the Congress was my home; I couldn't belong anywhere else but here.

Back in the Fold

When Dinesh Gundu Rao became the president of the Karnataka Congress, I rejoined the party in 2019. I am now a primary member of the Congress. I paid Rs 10 to re-enrol in the party that I first joined in 1979. My re-entry was quiet and I didn't want any fanfare because there were some old members who would have opposed it.

7

Anchored by My Family

MY FAMILY HAS been my anchor through all the choppy waters I have sailed on. When we got married, Hassan and I initially lived as part of a joint family with his parents and siblings. We moved out after a few years and set up our own home in Gulistan.

It is an old colonial bungalow, typical of old Bangalore and one of the few still standing in modern Bengaluru. My grandfather had purchased it for Rs 2,000 in 1924 and it was part of a trust that he had set up.

Hassan and I bought it from the trust and made our home here. We retained the heritage look and feel, and over the years we installed modern conveniences, but the renovations are subtly done. The garden is our place of joy, and this is where we have evening tea and chat about our day.

Hassan has a busy schedule with his real estate business; he still has an interest in the family business of Fazal's, Bengaluru's premier women's fashion destination store. The store began with his grandfather, Fazal Seth, who was the son of a chieftain from Mount Abu. He had fought with his family and moved to Bengaluru where he made his living as a hawker. He made his fortune by selling clothes to the Italian prisoners of war who were interned here during the Second World War. He made enough money from trading to set up Fazal & Sons.

His son, my father-in-law Hameed Fazal, inherited the business after him. He was a kind gentleman like his father and a complete contrast to his wife Hajra Fazal, who was a harridan. The only thing I had in common with my mother-in-law was smoking cigarettes and she was the one who got me started on this habit. She was a chain smoker, and family lore says that she couldn't abstain even on her wedding day when she was supposed to have popped out a pack of cigarettes from her dress and offered one to her husband, and said, 'Let's both smoke.' I believe it as she offered me a cigarette after Nooraine was born, and that's when I started to smoke.

A Strong Foundation

Our honeymoon trip cost Rs 139 for third-class tickets on Indian Railways as we set off on a tour around India. We could hop on and off wherever we wanted to; we visited Agra, Jaipur, Calcutta, Siliguri and many other places. I remember the 'wonder train' that took us up the scenic mountain route to Darjeeling; it had glass panes all around and I felt we could touch the Himalayas.

It was rough travel for a month, but I was able to adjust because of my public school and hostel training. In 1976, we had a second honeymoon; I sold a property that my father had gifted me, and

Hassan and I took off on a jaunt around the world for six whole months. We visited many countries including Turkey as well as Dubai, watched the Olympics in Canada and the bicentennial of the USA in New York. That was a brash and impulsive decision; we didn't know where the next penny was coming from, but we spent it all on the experience of a lifetime.

The basis of our marriage is love and trust. We have been married for 58 years. They have been good years, and Hassan is still the same loving, patient, and supportive man who fell in love with me; at the time of our marriage he was gawky looking but transformed from an ugly duckling into a swan. He has aged well and is still handsome. I am bold, impetuous, and independent; I used to travel to most places alone when I was in politics, but he never doubted me though I gave him plenty of reasons to do so. I have never crossed the *Lakshman Rekha* though I admit I loved the male attention that I got everywhere I went. I am very flirtatious by nature. When my brother Mathin complained that my name was linked to various men, my ever-loyal Hassan shut him up firmly. Hassan made me a woman of substance—all the credit goes to him for everything I have been able to do in life.

Wrong Place, Wrong Time

Hassan became a victim of circumstances and went through a very bad patch because of my political connections. When Gundu Rao became the Chief Minister of Karnataka in 1980, his long-time friend and trusted lieutenant, F.M. Khan, became the de facto CM. As far as I know, he didn't use his proximity and friendship to get any pecuniary gains. But he was on a power trip and was brazen about it. One day, in an inebriated state, F.M. Khan manhandled the Police Commissioner of Bengaluru, A.R. Nizamuddin, and the police never forgot this.

F.M. Khan had always been nice to me since the time I joined politics, he got along well with Hassan and had become a family friend. He used to visit our home very often, to the extent that it became his *adda* (hangout) in Bengaluru. Sometimes he overstayed his welcome and it was difficult to get him out. F.M. Khan's constant presence in our house had led to a slander campaign, with people linking us together. Perhaps because of the outgoing personality, gregarious and friendly nature with which the Almighty endowed me, my detractors tried to link me to many leaders in the state or even at the Centre. This bothered me initially but Hassan, ever protective, scotched the rumours and my acid tongue was a weapon I used liberally against anyone who tried to put me down.

F.M. Khan had fallen out of favour with the party high command and was expelled from the Congress in 1984, but my husband being a kind and gracious man continued to make him feel welcome at our house. This good nature would prove to be a disadvantage.

I have a sixth sense and I could smell danger. I had a premonition that we would need to brace ourselves for a time of turbulence. And it happened soon enough. After spending the evening with us, F.M. Khan left to meet his private secretary, S. Rajasekhar. Hassan decided to accompany him. It was the eve of Nooraine's 16th birthday, and I told him not to go with F.M. Khan but he went anyway.

The police had been looking for an excuse to get back at F.M. Khan for having misbehaved with the police commissioner in his hey days. They were waiting to get hold of him on some pretext that fateful day when Hassan went with him. But F.M. Khan somehow managed to slip away. Instead, they caught hold of my husband and hauled him to the police station. For a few hours, we didn't know where he had been taken, and by the time we got through to F.M. Khan, we learnt that Hassan was at the Munireddypalya police station. The incident was orchestrated by a police officer called B.M. Nagaraj on trumped-up charges.

F.M. Khan telephoned Deve Gowda, who was the No. 2 in the government; Chief Minister Ramakrishna Hegde was on one of his frequent nature cures. Gowda rang up the Commissioner and asked him to release Hassan but the police didn't comply. Nothing could stop the police from carrying out their vendetta against F.M. Khan. Hassan was stripped down to his underwear and was shivering in the damp cell. And all because he had accompanied F.M. Khan. His only fault was being in the wrong place at the wrong time with the wrong person. It was a miserable time for us, for the children and for the whole extended family, and we didn't know how to bail ourselves out from a situation that was not of our making.

My daughter Nishi's in-laws were very supportive at that time. My son-in-law, Rafu, a fine young man, hails from a *Nawab like* family in Ooty and stood by us. I was totally shattered by the turn of events. Never in my wildest imagination had I thought that we would have to undergo such torture. We fought the police allegations against Hassan tooth and nail in court; the legal battle went on for five years before we won. We stood by each other through it all.

Having endured this harrowing experience and being witness to my own ups and downs in politics, put my daughters off politics. In fact, no one in the family wants to be a politician, although Nooraine did once consider the possibility. Looking back, I realise that there are no permanent friends in politics. A friend today could become an enemy tomorrow. F.M. Khan had spotted my budding political career, but he also landed my husband in trouble. By the time I became a minister, he had become a toothless tiger, as anyone without power in politics becomes.

F.M. Khan's mother was admitted to the KR Hospital in Mysuru when I was the Minister for Medical Education. Her whole family visited her every day which was against hospital protocol. F.M. Khan did not heed the Medical Superintendent who complained to me. When I intervened, he was upset and said he would not rest until I was divested of my portfolio. He rejoiced when I was removed from the post and we never spoke to each other until his death.

Life is indeed strange. When Gundu Rao became the CM, Indira Gandhi had said that F.M. Khan was her third son because when she was out of power, he had hosted her at his estate and looked after her. F.M. Khan believed that Indira*ji* meant what she said and thought he would have her protection forever. But blood is thicker than water as he realised when he took on Rajiv Gandhi by putting up independent candidates in college union elections, against Congress party candidates. This was one of the reasons for his expulsion from the Congress.

Mea Culpa

I gave birth to our first child, our daughter Nishi, when I was 19 and our second daughter Nooraine at 23. I might as well admit it, like most women of my generation, I too was obsessed with having a son. I loved my two little daughters but I hankered for a boy. I wept when my second child was born because I hadn't given birth to a boy. It was not that I loved her less. I can never forget that she almost died when she was a baby. She had turned over her bed in the cradle and she was gasping for breath, almost choking. Holding her in my arms, I ran to Dr Sita Bhateja, one of the most reputed doctors, who saved her.

Some years after that, in 1979, I heard about a new technique in the West that was supposed to scientifically help conceive a male child. The Shettles method is based on the idea that male-producing sperm prefer alkaline conditions, whereas female-producing sperm prefer acidic conditions. I set off to London to meet a gynaecologist and find out more about the process.

I had barely landed there when Mrs Indira Gandhi pulled the rug from under Prime Minister Charan Singh's feet by withdrawing the Congress support. I came back at once to throw myself into the political scene. My career took precedence over my craving for a baby boy. That was many years ago, and over time, my thinking evolved.

However, much of our country is still in the hold of the patriarchal mindset which values a boy more than a girl. It reveals itself even in the names that people choose for their unwanted daughters. A recent report in the *Times of India* points out that in Rajasthan, across communities and castes, a second or a third daughter is unwelcome. They are given names such as *Dhapu* (meaning fed up), *Ramghani* (Ram, you have given us enough daughters), *Haichuki* (enough), *Antima* (last), the self-explanatory Missed Call, *Faltu* (wrong) to *Naraji* (anger). How is it with all the advances women have made in our country, people are still enamoured with sons over daughters!

I am proud of my two daughters who are compassionate, successful, independent, and strong. Both have chosen different paths. Nishi, my elder daughter, is a true Libran. She has two sons; she's easy-going, diplomatic and balances her life well. Her store on Cunningham Road in Bengaluru, Kahawa – The Design Store, was a platform for upcoming designers and artists to showcase their art, clothes, jewellery, pottery, homeware and more. Nishi is the go-to person in the family, community and for friends alike, for anything that needs organising, or if someone is unwell or needs help. She's there for people in need like Florence Nightingale.

My younger daughter Nooraine co-founded Inventure Academy, which is now ranked #1 in Karnataka and South India, and amongst the top 5 K12 (kindergarten to 12th grade) schools all India. The school is aimed at enabling every learner to be the best possible version of themselves, and contribute to a better world. Inventure has also adopted a government school in Whitefield which is fast emerging as a Public-Private Partnership (PPP) model for quality education in government schools. Prior to this, she worked with Reuters for nine years in several countries after her MBA from Boston University. The girl who used to give me a scare by zooming around on a motorbike from the age of 13 has grown into a renowned educationist and shapes the lives of thousands of children through her commitment to create the much-needed changemakers.

At one point, Nooraine considered entering politics. She, however, chose to focus on working actively in transforming education in India. The exposure she got from my political career and her own world experiences are helpful especially when she works collaboratively with the government to influence policy and improve the quality of education. She doesn't hesitate to hold the Karnataka government accountable on matters such as ban on online education during the pandemic in 2020, the irresponsible knee-jerk decisions on school fees and poor public and social infrastructure. She's pitched in on such issues by going to court, holding peaceful marches or highlighting issues in the media.

I'm happy that both my daughters have learnt invaluable life lessons from my own journey, and have imbibed their father's patience and kindness too.

I have had a few pregnancies terminated medically during the course of my career. This was a decision that I took after due thought, and I think every woman should have the right to make this choice. I was taken aback and disappointed when the USA, the self-styled leader of the free world, denied this right to women by making abortion illegal.

There was a hilarious turn of events when Nishi was pregnant with her first child Shariq. The ultrasound tests indicated the baby was a girl and when Nishi gave birth, it turned out to be a boy! I fainted with shock which the family found hilarious. We call him a miracle child!

Hassan became a besotted grandfather when our first grandson was born. We used to go abroad with my younger daughter Nooraine annually, and Hassan would insist on taking Shariq along though he was a little boy of three. It was a torture for the little boy getting up at odd hours to catch the flights. He would bawl his lungs out, kicking and screaming in protest. But Hassan could not bear to be parted from our grandson and brought him along everywhere we went. Shariq, 32 now, is a budding entrepreneur who is focusing on combining his twin passions for lifestyle and design. He has established a brand called Life Behind Bars (LBB) and is an upcoming graffiti artist. His younger brother Ryaan, a graduate from Inventure Academy and Sports Management & Science, University of Nottingham Trent, is currently working in the United Kingdom on a student work visa. His biggest strength is his ability to connect with people and help them. Hassan and I were hands-on parents and spent a lot of time with our daughters. We would organise their birthday parties for which I would bake the cake and ice it myself. On Sundays, we took them to the drive-in theatre to see movies and spent time bonding as a family. We would take them to Cubbon Park for a joy ride in the toy train, and to the Lalbagh glass house for the superb annual flower shows, and Hassan's fashion shows.

I dressed the girls in identical clothes, backcombed their hair and made them look adorable. Hassan is an ace photographer and would follow them with a video camera and record them while they enacted fairy tales.

When they were younger, Nooraine was timid and scared of her own shadow. She was deeply affected by the character assassination that I experienced. She would overhear my brother's complaints about the rumours about me, and as a child of eight, she was affected by talk of my relationships and she hated the sight of F.M. Khan. Nishi seemed to handle it better, and played the role of a responsible older sibling and was always there for Nooraine. I too always looked out for my younger brothers and sister.

Now there are two of us; my brother Ameen Rahaman owned a packaging unit, Ficus Pax. He now deals with eco-friendly products and is doing brilliantly. He is an affectionate brother.

Tragic Accident

Sadly, my youngest brother and sister have passed on.

My beautiful younger sister Nadira married Hassan's cousin, Jameel. She was ill for many years with lupus and died at 60. Mathin died just after his 50th birthday, in 2002. He turned 50 in July and on my birthday on 4th November, he was gone. I had a premonition that something was going to go wrong, and for a month before my brother's death, I was very uneasy, but I couldn't understand why.

Elton John had performed at the Palace Grounds in Bengaluru on 2 November, and I had gotten him passes for the show as he was a big fan. After attending the concert, my brother and his friends partied the whole night and early the next morning they left for Goa. I did not have a clue that they had left for Goa; there was a party planned for my birthday that evening at home. I was in my chambers in Vidhana Soudha, on the second-floor room performing Lakshmi Puja for Deepavali, when my niece called me. She said Mathin had been in a car accident.

My assistant called the Dharwad police who said Mathin had been found alive and was taken to the hospital. But he didn't survive. He had been conscious after the accident and handed over his mobile to a police constable as he lay on the road for 20 minutes. I did not know how to break the news to my mother because she would be distraught. Prema *Akka* and SMK helped with getting the body back.

The Brother I Found

After Mathin's passing away, Irfan Razack took his place in my heart and family. He is the chairman of Prestige Group and I regard him as my kid brother. We belong to the same community of Cutchi Memons, and over a period of time, have developed a great bond. His wife Badar is like my younger sister.

Irfan is a great philanthropist and is like the godfather who helps the poor and needy in the community. This is what I appreciate

Growing Up Years

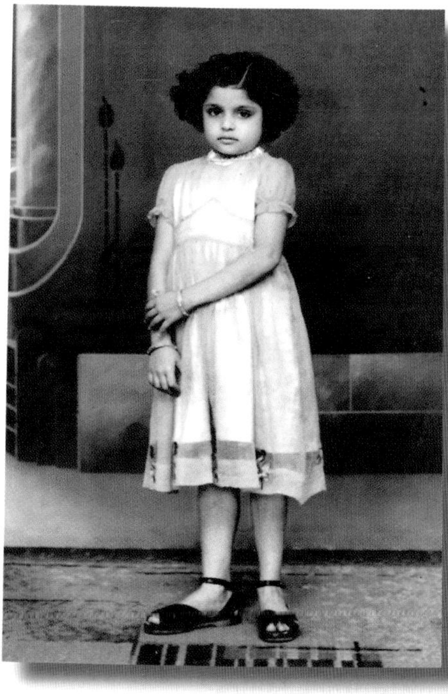

(Clockwise from top left):
The author as a child with her *Mamu* (her mother's brother); with her brother Ameen and a cousin sister; at age 5; and with permed hair before being admitted as boarder to the Lawrence School in Lovedale

With Tibetan spiritual leader the Dalai Lama and cardio surgeon Dr Devi Shetty (right) at a public function in Bangalore

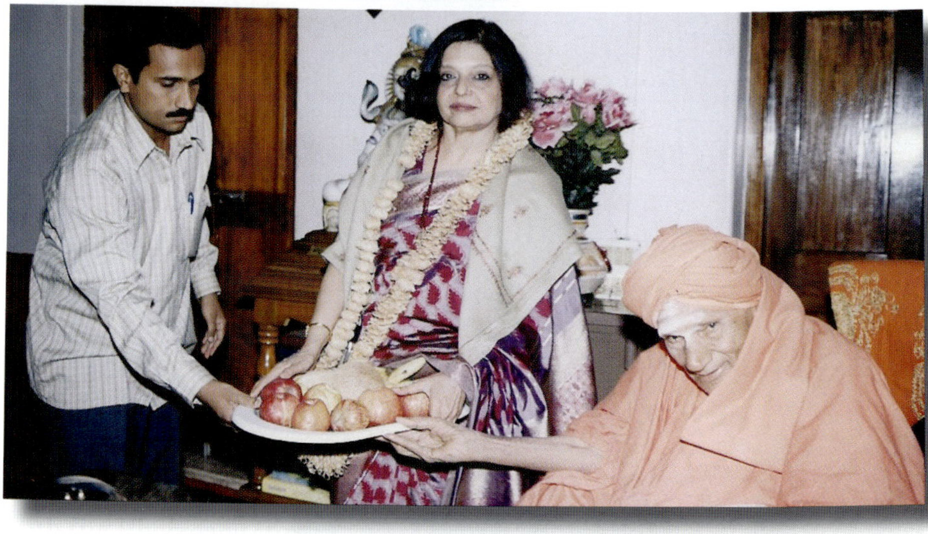

The author receiving blessings from Shivakumara Swami*ji* of Sree Siddaganga Matha in Tumkur district, Karnataka in 2003

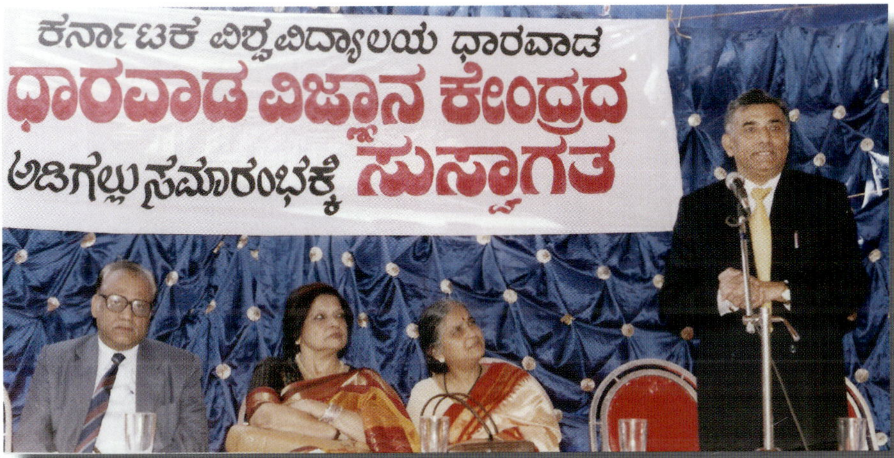

With educator and author Sudha Murthy at the foundation stone laying ceremony for a Science City at Dharwad in 2004. She was the Science and Technology Minister then

The author (third from right) with Mysore Maharaja Srikantadatta Narasimharaja Wadiyar (centre), DPS Whitefield vice-chairperson Annabelle (third from left), actor Ambareesh (second from left), former Minister Arun Ladd (left) and Prema Krishna (right) in Bangalore during her husband's 70th birthday celebrations in 2010

With former Union Minister Mani Shankar Aiyar at her residence in Bengaluru in 2018

The author with current Karnataka CM Basavaraj Bommai (second from left), former CM S.M. Krishna (centre), his wife Prema and former minister R.V. Deshpande's son Prasad (right) at Deshpande's golden wedding anniversary celebrations in Bengaluru in 2022

A Sports Enthusiast

With former tennis ace Vijay Amritraj at Windsor Manor, Bangalore

The author at Wimbledon in London in 2019

With legendary cricketer Kapil Dev, her daughter Nooraine and her brother Irfan Razack at Inventure Graduation Day 2021

Family & Friends

(LEFT): With her husband Hassan's grandmother.
The author's mother Rukhiya blessing her when she became an MLC of the Karnataka Assembly in 1994

With husband Hassan, and daughters Nishi and Nooraine

Daughters Nishi and Nooraine when they were 7 and 3 years old, respectively

With husband Hassan (left), brother Ameen Rahaman (second from right), and friend Saroj Bagaria

With friends Manju Shah (left) and Shehnaz Sait (centre), and actor Shabana Azmi in Bengaluru in April 2020

The author with her daughters Nishi and Nooraine and grandsons Shariq and Ryaan on her 70th birthday in Bengaluru

(Clockwise from top left): The author with husband Hassan, daughters Nishi and Nooraine, and Jitu during the wedding of Jitu's son Karan in Bengaluru in 2021

Old friends Roshan Sripad (right) and Saroj Bagaria at the author's house

The author with lawyer Divya Balagopal (left), Nooraine, dermatologist Dr Chytra Anand and Tasneem, former Reuters executive, at her house

(L-R): Hassan Fazal, Tasneem, Lina (Jitu's wife), Asma, Almas and the author at the Diwali celebrations hosted by Jitu

The author's grand puppies (L-R) Raksha, Mia, Talia and Tasha

about him. Subsequently, he and my younger daughter Nooraine co-founded an international day school Inventure Academy, now ranked #1 in Karnataka.

The Son I Never Had

I had always hankered for a son and I found him in Sonny aka Jitu Virwani. He is compassionate, loving and caring. He has a great sense of humour and is a philanthropist as well. He's helped almost 50 government schools, and done commendable work to improve the city's infrastructure in the PPP space.

Though he's very busy as chairman of the Embassy Group, he always makes time for me, and his WhatsApp exchanges are precious to me. Wherever in the world we are, he never forgets to WhatsApp me 'Good morning mama' and I reply, 'Good morning, sonny'. His wife Leena is an adorable person and gets along well with my daughters and me. I am truly blessed to have these people in my life. It's important to cultivate a strong supportive circle of friends and well-wishers. I still maintain a warm relationship with my childhood friends.

I had a small apartment where I used to entertain my friends, as Hassan would not agree to card games being played or alcohol being served in our family home. For years, I played rummy with my friends at different clubs. I persuaded Hassan to learn to play golf and become a member of the Bangalore Golf Club, so I could host card sessions when it was my turn. The poor fellow struggled and learnt to play golf and became a member of the BGC. The biggest joke is that I have stopped playing card games, but Hassan still enjoys his game of golf.

Multitasking

I am a multitasker and have kept myself busy with many interests. I am always well-groomed because I have an inherent flair for designing. I was lucky that I could get the best materials from the family store Fazal's. I loved posing for the camera too and was a fashion trendsetter. When my girls were babies, I used to design their clothes. Their clothes would have frills, beads, and tassels and I would dress them up like little dolls. Even as a judge of the consumer disputes redressal court, I kept up with my interest in designing clothes.

Margaret Alva appointed me as the first woman judge of the Bengaluru District Consumer Disputes Redressal Forum. After I finished at the Consumer Forum, I used to go to Fazal's and design clothes. My signature style is chiffons and georgettes and crepes because they drape well. When I became a minister, I bought a whole lot of *Kanjeevaram* sarees to wear to the many events I attended. I only needed five minutes to get ready; I didn't wear much make-up, all I needed was a dash of my favourite pink lipstick.

I became a very good cook though I didn't like it when my mother and later my mother-in-law forced me to cook at a young age. Later I began experimenting in the kitchen and tried out innovative recipes. My signature dish is tandoori chicken. It is a recipe that I came out with. I did not follow any book or learn it from my mother or my grandmother or anybody. I just experimented and everybody loved it. There was a time when I would sit and barbecue 20 chickens when we went to Nandi Hills (near Bengaluru) for a picnic as a family. I was very good at making desserts and I used to make a dessert called *pusee which* is a typically Muslim dessert, full of *khova* (dried/thickened milk for Indian dessert), badam (almonds), pista (pistachios), and eggs.

After kissing politics goodbye, I made a foray into the jewellery line as I have a passion for all beautiful things. Curating jewellery is my stress buster. I converted a room in my bungalow into a jewellery studio called 'The Private Collection by Naf'. Naf is short for my name.

At boarding school, I learned horse riding. I took piano lessons too and appeared for the Royal Trinity exam in music and theory, but I didn't keep up with my practice. I am an ardent sports buff though; I love tennis, football and cricket and follow all the matches avidly.

Work-Life Balance

I wanted to show that women could also succeed in a man's world and ensure that no man treated me like my father did my mother.

For women, even in today's age, there are fewer opportunities, more obstacles and more responsibilities. Despite being a career woman, one has to juggle being a homemaker and most importantly a mother. This is the general scenario for all women. Without family support it's impossible to be a career woman, especially in politics which is a cesspool, and it's getting murkier as only money and muscle power are important. Though a few women have shattered the glass ceiling in their respective careers, we are considered to be the weaker sex. Our ability to perform is always questioned. It's not a level playing field for men and women which is improper. There's definitely discrimination between men and women and there's no equality.

Even in the 21st century, rapes are rampant which is barbaric and shameful. Drunken husbands abuse and beat their wives. I'm emphasising that courage and family support from husband and children are the crux for a successful career. Be courageous and face adversity.

For those girls with political ambitions or those who are career-oriented, you have to be thick-skinned as character assassination is the only weapon men have against the fair sex. Don't be despondent or throw in the towel, fight to achieve your goal on your own terms. It was worse for me being a Muslim and a woman, as there were very few Muslim women in politics. My own community nipped my career a decade earlier as they thought a woman's place was at home and not in politics, and this despite my achievements! They would pick on me for trivial things such as my anglicized accent in Kannada – they did this as I was not corrupt and couldn't frame charges. My only aim to join politics was to emulate my idol Indira Gandhi in my own small way, and contribute to the upliftment of women and the less privileged. By denying me the opportunity to grow further in politics, the Congress lost an opportunity to project a more progressive inclusive woman as the face of the community. But I have persevered in my philosophy that 'Service to mankind is Service to God'.

Sometimes younger people struggle for a work-life balance, and ask me how I was and am still able to do the many things that I do. I have been a hands-on mother and a good homemaker. Despite my busy schedule, I went to my kids' school when necessary to discuss their progress with the teachers. I made it a point to keep Sundays as much as possible for the family and spent it doing activities that all of us – my husband, daughters and I – could enjoy together.

But it's always a struggle to get the balance right and everything comes at a cost.

Here's how I learnt to juggle my professional and personal life. The key tips for success: time and budget management. Time management is my mantra: One should never be late for appointments and must always respect others' time. It's the key to completing chores or projects on time.

Similarly, one should always plan a budget and stick to it. People would ask me how I was able to handle the budgets of the government departments that I headed. I learnt to run an efficient home and I applied the same principles at work. If you can budget your home, you can run any team or department efficiently.

Though I didn't complete my college education, I taught myself everything that I needed to know. Perhaps, it would have been easier had I been formally educated. Hence I am a stronger believer of the saying that 'when you educate a woman, you educate a nation'.

Afterword

MY LIFE NOW has a very different rhythm. The house is quieter. The demands on the time of a retired politician are not as intense. I continue to get requests from people to write recommendation letters or attend events, though they are fewer than before. I do the first unhesitatingly and I try to drop in for a brief while at weddings and birthdays as my health is not at its best.

Most of my time is dedicated to social work. Through a foundation I established, called KARE, I get help from notable people like Dr Devi Shetty, a world-renowned cardiac surgeon and the Founder and Chairman of Narayana Health. Thanks to his invaluable support, we are able to help provide neonatal care for babies and cardiac patients. I started the foundation soon after my mother died 11 years ago. She was a pious woman and I wanted to do something to honour her. I don't believe in giving any donations for marriages; I give financial aid for the education and medical expenses of poor children.

I know the directors of leading government hospitals and I reach out to them to help people who can't afford to pay for their treatment. I help with school fees, uniforms, and books. This is the kind of work I love to do; it gives me purpose in life. I am also a life member of a Muslim orphanage.

I follow politics; I see what's trending on Twitter. Sometimes, I am amused by the political posturings as I know the truth behind it all. I do miss being in the thick of things. It was always my cherished dream to be in politics. I would still choose politics because it connects me with people. I did not want to make money through my political positions or clout because I had enough. I went into politics to help people.

I never aspired to be on the national level of politics. Unlike many others who sought such positions, I was happy to be recognised in my city and state. There are other people like me in state politics who don't get into politics at the Central or national levels because there we would be small fish in a big ocean, one among 800-odd MPs. In your state, you are very well recognised, and that's why I was never interested in Delhi politics. Why would I want to go and live in an MP's flat in Delhi when I have my home here? I would rather be a big fish in a small pond.

This is the stage of life where one asks, 'Has it been a satisfactory life?' There are many more things I could have accomplished had I continued in politics, I'm sure of that. I had a baptism by fire and my journey in politics has been thorny. My haughtiness and my temper have, at times, got the better of me and they cost me positions that were within my reach. My loyalty to my mentors has also worked against me, oddly enough. The lack of support to progressive women from established male political leaders in my community has not enabled women like me to succeed either.

Despite the several disappointments in my career, I wouldn't choose to live a different life. My life has been rich in experiences; I have dined with the mightiest and the humblest and met people from varied walks of life. I think I have been able to do a bit of good in the world, as a politician, a social worker, a home maker and a human being.

To accomplish anything in life, you must first dream, then you must convert the dream into a vision, and finally, turn the vision into reality. I had a dream at the age of 13 that I wanted to be in politics. I converted that dream into a vision and the vision into reality.

You've got to have character and grit, you have to catch the bull by the horns and rise to the occasion. I got through by sheer grit, hard work, and luck of the draw. And I never gave up.

I'm a fighter and a survivor.

Nafees Fazal as Friends & Family See Her

I have had the pleasure of knowing Nafees for the last 25 years. My first encounter with her was during her tenure as Medical Education Minister and my early days as a practicing cardiologist. We had a very formal relationship at that period. But since then we have become great friends and she used to try to teach me medicine and I very clearly told her that was my field as much as politics was hers.

She is a wonderful multifaceted personality and combines her public duties with being a great wife, mother, grandmother and friend to the world. Her opinions are always in the open and never camouflaged.

Radha and me have had the pleasure of being friends of the family and helped see the world through her eyes and learn from it.

Dr Ranganath Nayak
Senior Consultant Cardiologist, Manipal Hospital

Nafees Fazal has written her memoir *Breaking Barriers*. It's an appropriate title for her biography.

I always address Nafees as 'Appa' and I have a lot of respect for her frank and gutsy attitude. At a time when not many ladies, for that matter none at all from the Cutchi Memon community ventured into public life, she pursued politics with a passion. It is only her clean-headed thinking, forthright attitude, and passion she had in public life that made her reach the heights of being a Minister in the cabinet of the Government of Karnataka, under the Chief Ministership of Mr S.M. Krishna. She did full justice to her portfolio as Medical Education Minister and was quick to get into the grips of the situation and learnt the details of her responsibility as a Minister and got herself updated, so she could not be pushed around. She has a strong personality with a never-say-die attitude if she wants to do something. She is endowed with intelligence and common sense which got her to where she did.

She is a great cook and superlative homemaker, highly affectionate, caring, and thoughtful to all her friends and relatives. Overall, I would describe *Naffapa* as a coconut. Hard on the exterior but soft and sweet on the inside.

I'm sure her story will be an inspiration to all readers, especially to women, who will get inspired to create their own identities.

Irfan Razack
Chairman & Managing Director, Prestige Group

I consider Ms Nafees Fazal as my second mother. Over the years I have known her, she has remained a shining example of determination and fortitude. As a strong believer in the power of giving back to the communities around us, I hold a deep admiration for her compassion and illustrious career marked by standing up for what's right. Inspirational and pioneering, this book will give you an intimate insight into the power of following your dreams and breaking barriers. Kudos!

Jitu Virwani
Chairman & Managing Director, Embassy Group

Nafees Fazal, my wife, is fearless, bold, and principled. She does what she thinks is right, and if she gets into trouble by being frank, as an expert politician, she will convince the world she is right! She is large-hearted; people flock often to ask for help and she obliges all of them. I feel that she should have married Santa Claus, as the whole time she is giving away money and possessions. She's also an expert cook and wins over everyone with her samosas and biryani.

Hassan Fazal

I happen to be the younger brother of Nafees Fazal. There is a lot you can say about my sister which I admire! She is a classy, beautiful intellectual with a very good sense of humour.

She has clarity and vision in whatever she does and is highly dedicated. She is fearless and reaches her target in whatever she wants to do.

She has a heart of gold and is kind and compassionate to the poor and helps people across caste, creed, and religion!

She may be one of a few Muslim women who have become a minister in the state of Karnataka. She fought against all odds to become a minister and is a woman of substance. She leads two lives, one as a mother and grandmother who gives love to her family, and the other as a truly dedicated professional who believes in what she does and gives back to society.

She is my best buddy and we discuss all the topics which are of interest. I share my thoughts and respect her advice as she is mature and is like a tigress when she has to be one.

AMEEN RAHAMAN

The first time I read the draft of Mama's book, tears streamed down my face uncontrollably as I truly understood my mother's journey and perils for the very first time. I was finally able to comprehend her single-minded determination to become a minister, her inability to take no for answer, and her need for admiration irrespective of the consequences on her or her family.

I also cried tears of happiness at the realisation that this little girl went on to become South India's first woman Muslim Minister in Independent India.

Talk about breaking all barriers!

The little girl was of course my mother who I have always deeply loved, even when as a child I stuttered and stammered around her, and would on occasion be upset by her unconventional life choices.

She pursued her dreams while being a devoted, but sometimes absent mother. A mother who admirably juggled the demands of a challenging political career and being a 'mama' to my sister and me. She has always been here for us when we absolutely needed her, unconditional in her love and support for all our adventures and ventures.

Breaking Barriers is a story about a woman who has made it against all odds! Don't let the silver spoon she was born with or the scale of her ambition or achievements fool you. The story of a highly complex kid who grew into a powerful politician and still retains the vulnerable little girl in her is a must-read.

Why should you read it? Well, firstly it's an amazing story of a woman who juggled her multiple roles in a highly complex society, a conservative community and a challenging world of Indian politics, told in a very relatable way. It's also a book about a life fully lived with all the ups and downs and learning that life offers us.

I hope this book will inspire women across the spectrum to dream and pursue their dreams while being mindful of the impact of their choices on their family and nation.

I pray that this book will help our political and community leaders ask themselves some hard questions and enable other women who want to contribute to the betterment of society.

And I hope my beautiful, inspirational and loving mother in telling her story will finally heal and recognise all that she has achieved and should be grateful for.

NOORAINE FAZAL

Founding Managing Trustee & CEO, Inventure Academy

Bibliography

'1999 India General Elections Results'. *elections.in*. https://www.elections.in/parliamentary-constituencies/1999-election-results.html

'Cost of dismissing Veerendra Patil'. *The Hindu*, 27 April 2018. https://www.thehindu.com/news/national/karnataka/cost-of-dismissing-veerendra-patil/article23688341.ece

'Diagnosis of a Riot'. *The City TAB*, 15 April 1984.

'Kaveri River water dispute'. *Wikipedia*.

'Lok Sabha Election Results 2019'. *elections.in*. https://www.elections.in/indian-general-election/2019/

'The Muslim Women (Protection of Rights on Marriage) Bill, 2019.' *PRS Legislative Research*. https://prsindia.org/billtrack/the-muslim-women-protection-of-rights-on-marriage-bill-2019

'UPA report card: Nine years, nine scams'. *India Today Gallery*, 22 May 2013. https://www.indiatoday.in/india/photo/upa-govt-9-years-9-scams-sonia-manmohan-369868-2013-05-22

Aiyar, Mani Shankar. 'Working with Rajiv Gandhi' (Book review). *The Hindu*, 2 January 2021. https://www.thehindu.com/books/books-reviews/my-years-with-rajiv-review-working-with-rajiv-gandhi/article33472403.ece

Alva, Margaret. *Courage & Commitment: An Autobiography*. New Delhi: Rupa Publications, 2016

Ananth, V. Krishna. *India Since Independence: Making Sense of Indian Politics.* New Delhi: Pearson India, 2010.

Barman, Abheek. '2014 Lok Sabha Elections Results: How the Congress messed up its chances'. *The Economic Times*, 16 May 2014. https://economictimes.indiatimes.com/news/politics-and-nation/2014-lok-sabha-elections-results-how-the-congress-messed-up-its-chances/articleshow/35215846.cms?from=mdr

Baru, Sanjaya. *1991: How P.V. Narasimha Rao Made History*. New Delhi: Aleph Book Company, 2016.

Chengappa, Raj. 'Janata Party registers convincing victory in Karnataka civic elections.' *India Today*, 18 July 2013. https://www.indiatoday.in/magazine/indiascope/story/19830831-janata-party-registers-convincing-victory-in-karnataka-civic-elections-770943-2013-07-18

Connelly, Matthew. 'Controlling Passions'. *The Wilson Quarterly* vol. 32(3), 2008. http://www.jstor.org/stable/40262142

Dinakar, C. *Veerappan's Prize Catch: Rajkumar*. New Delhi: Konark Publishers, 2003.

Dutta, Prabhash K. 'Kargil: How Bofors guns made Pakistan eat humble pie'. *India Today*, 26 July 2019. https://www.indiatoday.in/news-analysis/story/bofors-the-controversial-gun-that-won-kargil-war-for-india-1573814-2019-07-26

Ehrlich, Paul R. *The Population Bomb*. New York: Sieera Club-Ballantine Book, 1968.

Eliazer Nelson, Ann Raeboline Lincy, Kavitha Ravichandran & Usha Antony. 'The impact of the Green Revolution on indigenous crops of India'. *Journal of Ethnic Foods* vol. 6, Article No. 8 (2019). https://doi.org/10.1186/s42779-019-0011-9

ET Now Digital. '1947: India in numbers – What was the country's GDP, population, per-capita income?' *Times Now News*, 14 August 2020. https://www.timesnownews.com/business-economy/economy/article/1947-india-in-numbers-what-was-the-country-s-gdp-population-per-capita-income/636908

Express Web Desk. 'What is Shah Bano case?' *The Indian Express*, 23 August 2017. https://indianexpress.com/article/what-is/what-is-shah-bano-case-4809632/

FPJ Web Desk. 'Top 5 achievements during Manmohan Singh's tenure as Prime Minister of India'. *The Free Press Journal*, 26 September 2019. https://www.freepressjournal.in/india/top-5-achievements-during-manmohan-singhs-tenure-as-prime-minister-of-india

Ghosh, Poulomi. 'G-23 is not Ji Huzoor 23: Sibal's dig at high command amid Punjab row, says Congress has no president'. *Hindustan Times*, 29 September 2021. https://www.hindustantimes.com/india-news/there-is-no-president-don-t-know-who-is-taking-decision-kapil-sibal-on-punjab-crisis-101632912518246.html

Ghosh, Poulomi. 'Shashi Tharoor supports Kapil Sibal, says he fought many legal battles for Congress'. *Hindustan Times*, 30 September 2021. https://www.hindustantimes.com/india-news/shashi-tharoor-supports-kapil-sibal-says-he-fought-many-legal-battles-for-congress-101633004866080.html

Gupte, Prajakta R. 'India: "The Emergency" and the Politics of Mass Sterilization'. *Education About Asia* vol. 22:3 (Winter 2017): Demographics, Social Policy, and Asia, Part I. https://www.asianstudies.org/publications/eaa/archives/india-the-emergency-and-the-politics-of-mass-sterilization/

Habibullah, Wajahat. *My Years with Rajiv: Triumph and Tragedy*. Chennai: Westland, 2020.

Kulshrestha, Parul. 'From Phaltu to Antima to Missed Call: The curious case of naming girls in Rajasthan'. *The Times of India*, 13 December 2021. https://timesofindia.indiatimes.com/india/from-phaltu-to-antima-to-missed-call-the-curious-case-of-naming-girls-in-rajasthan/articleshow/88206798.cms

Kumar, C.B. Yeshwanth & Binoo K. John. 'Hasty imposition of President's Rule in Karnataka forces Congress (I) to close ranks'. *India Today*, 31 October 1990. https://www.indiatoday.in/magazine/special-report/story/19901031-hasty-imposition-of-presidents-rule-in-karnataka-forces-congressi-to-close-ranks-813213-1990-10-31

Malhotra, Inder. 'The abrupt end of Emergency'. Opinion, *The Indian Express*, 4 August 2014. https://indianexpress.com/article/opinion/columns/the-abrupt-end-of-emergency/

Mantri, Geetika. 'Explained: What the Cauvery water dispute between Karnataka and TN is all about'. *The News Minute*, 15 February 2018. https://www.thenewsminute.com/article/explained-what-cauvery-water-dispute-between-karnataka-and-tn-all-about-76528

Mathew, George (ed.). *Shift in Indian Politics: 1983 Elections in Andhra Pradesh and Karnataka*. New Delhi: Concept Publishing Co., 1984.

McCoy, Terrence. 'The forgotten roots of India's mass sterilization program'. *The Washington Post*, 15 November 2014. https://www.washingtonpost.com/news/morning-mix/wp/2014/11/14/the-malthusian-roots-of-indias-mass-sterilization-program/

Mehta, Vinod. *The Sanjay Story: From Anand Bhavan To Amethi*. First published in 1978. New Delhi: HarperCollins, 2012.

Menon, Parvathi. 'Dowry Deaths in Bangalore'. *Frontline* 16 (17), 14-27 August 1999, pp. 64-73.

Nilekani, Nandan. *Imagining India: Ideas for the New Century*. New Delhi: Penguin, 2009.

Pitroda, Sam. 'We lost Rajiv Gandhi and we lost him to lies'. *The Week*, 30 May 2021. https://www.theweek.in/theweek/cover/2021/05/20/we-lost-rajiv-gandhi-and-we-lost-him-to-lies--writes-sam-pitroda.html

Prasad, Ravi Visvesvaraya Sharada. 'Multiple narratives exist for why Indira Gandhi lifted the Emergency', Opinion, *The Indian Express*, 23 February 2019. https://indianexpress.com/article/opinion/columns/emergency-chronicles-indira-gandhi-5597323/

PTI. 'Abdul Kareem Telgi: From a vegetable vendor to scam mastermind'. *The Economic Times,* 26 October 2017. https://economictimes.indiatimes.com/news/politics-and-nation/abdul-kareem-telgi-from-a-vegetable-vendor-to-scam-mastermind/articleshow/61248396.cms?from=mdr

PTI. 'Kannada actor Rajkumar dies of heart attack'. *The Times of India*, 13 April 2006. https://timesofindia.indiatimes.com/entertainment/hindi/bollywood/news/kannada-actor-rajkumar-dies-of-heart-attack/articleshow/1487948.cms

PTI. 'WEF's gender gap index: India slips 28 places, ranks 140 among 156 countries'. *The Hindu*, 31 March 2021. https://www.thehindu.com/news/national/wefs-gender-gap-index-india-slips-28-places-ranks-140-among-156-countries/article34206867.ece

Raghavan, R.K. *A Road Well Travelled: An Autobiography*. Chennai: Westland, 2020

Sachar Committee Report. Ministry of Minority Affairs, GOI. https://minorityaffairs.gov.in/reports/sachar-committee-report

Singh, D.K. 'From Shah Bano to Shayara Bano: The evolution of Indian society and polity'. *Hindustan Times*, 23 August 2017. https://www.hindustantimes.com/india-news/from-shah-bano-to-shayara-bano-the-evolution-of-indian-society-and-polity/story-S9VYNxOdYIdVHTYSejDw5L.html

Sreenivas, Mytheli. 'Population Bomb? The Debate over Indian Population'. *The Ohio State University*. 2009 https://origins.osu.edu/article/population-bomb-debate-over-indian-population?

Suri, Sanjay. *1984: The Anti-Sikh Riots and After*. New Delhi: HarperCollins, 2015.

Thakur, Aksheev and Ralph Alex Arakal. 'Fatwas are interpretations of Quran, not diktats: Nafees Fazal'. *Deccan Chronicle*, 22 October 2017. https://www.deccanchronicle.com/nation/in-other-news/221017/fatwas-are-interpretations-of-quran-not-diktats-nafees-fazal.html

Thakur, Atul. 'Literacy rate for Muslims worse than SC/STs'. *The Times of India*, 13 August 2020. https://timesofindia.indiatimes.com/india/literacy-rate-for-muslims-worse-than-sc/sts/articleshow/77514868.cms

TNN. 'Bangalore to have Science City in 5 years'. *The Times of India*, 16 December 2002. https://timesofindia.indiatimes.com/city/bengaluru/bangalore-to-have-science-city-in-5-years/articleshow/31499124.cms

TNN. 'CWC meet: Gandhi loyalists view G-23 letter as revolt, crush call for change'. *The Times of India*, 25 August 2020. https://timesofindia.indiatimes.com/india/cwc-meet-gandhi-loyalists-view-g-23-letter-as-revolt-crush-call-for-change/articleshow/77731417.cms

Upadhya, Ramakrishna. *Natak Karnatak*. New Delhi: Prarthana Books, 2011.

Web Desk. 'When Power Star's father Rajkumar was abducted by forest brigand Veerappan'. *India Today*, 29 October 2021.

https://www.indiatoday.in/movies/regional-cinema/story/when-power-star-s-father-rajkumar-was-abducted-by-forest-brigand-veerappan-1871084-2021-10-29

Zaidi, S. Hussain and Brijesh Singh. *Dangerous Minds: Eight Riveting Profiles of Homegrown Terrorists*. New Delhi: Penguin Random House, 2018.

Appendices

ವೈದ್ಯಕೀಯ ಶಿಕ್ಷಣ ಸಚಿವೆ ನಫೀಸಾ ಫಾಜಲ್ ಅವರಿಂದು ವಿಕ್ಟೋರಿಯಾ ಆಸ್ಪತ್ರೆಯ ಸುಟ್ಟ ಗಾಯಗಳ ವಿಭಾಗಕ್ಕೆ ಅನಿರೀಕ್ಷಿತ ಭೇಟಿ ನೀಡಿದರು.

ವಿಕ್ಟೋರಿಯಾ ಆಸ್ಪತ್ರೆ ಹಿರಿಯ ಅಧಿಕಾರಿಗಳ ಸಭೆಗೆ ಸಚಿವೆ ಆದೇಶ

ಬೆಂಗಳೂರು, ಅ. ೨೪- ವೈದ್ಯಕೀಯ ಶಿಕ್ಷಣ ರಾಜ್ಯ ಸಚಿವೆ ನಫೀಜ ಫಜಲ್ ಅವರು ರಾಜ್ಯ ವಿಧಾನಸಭೆ ಅಧಿವೇಶನ ನಂತರ ವಿಕ್ಟೋಯಾ ಆಸ್ಪತ್ರೆಯ ಹಿರಿಯ ವೈದ್ಯರು ಹಾಗೂ ಅಧಿಕಾರಿಗಳ ಸಭೆಯನ್ನು ಕರೆದಿದ್ದಾರೆ.

ಆಸ್ಪತ್ರೆಗೆ ಅನಿರೀಕ್ಷಿತ ಭೇಟಿ ನೀಡಿ ಪರಿಶೀಲಿಸಿದ ನಂತರ ಸುದ್ದಿಗಾರರಿಗೆ ಈ ವಿಷಯ ತಿಳಿಸಿದರು.

ಆಸ್ಪತ್ರೆಯಲ್ಲಿ ರೋಗಿಗಳಿಗೆ ನೀಡುತ್ತಿರುವ ಸೇವೆ ಬಗ್ಗೆ ತಮಗೆ ಅಸಮಾಧಾನ ಎದೆ ಎಂದ ಅವರು ಆಸ್ಪತ್ರೆಗೆ ಅವಶ್ಯವಾಗಿ ಬೇಕಾದ ಹಣದ ನೆರವು ಇತ್ಯಾದಿ ಸಮಸ್ಯೆಗಳ ಬಗ್ಗೆ ಈ ಸಭೆಯಲ್ಲಿ ಚರ್ಚಿಸಲಾಗುವುದು ಎಂದು ತಿಳಿಸಿದರು.

ಆಸ್ಪತ್ರೆಗೆ ತೆರಳುವ ಮುಖ್ಯ ದ್ವಾರದಲ್ಲಿ ಬಿ.ಎಂ.ಟಿ.ಸಿ. ಬಸ್ಸುಗಳನ್ನು ಯದ್ವಾತದ್ವಾ ನಿಲ್ಲಿಸಲಾಗುತ್ತಿದೆ. ಇದರಿಂದ ತುರ್ತು ಚಿಕಿತ್ಸೆ ಪಡೆಯುವ ರೋಗಿಗಳು ಆಸ್ಪತ್ರೆಗೆ ತೆರಳಲು ಕಷ್ಟವಾಗುತ್ತಿದೆ. ಈ ಬಗ್ಗೆಯು ಸಾರಿಗೆ ಅಧಿಕಾರಿಗಳ ಜತೆ ಚರ್ಚಿಸುವುದಾಗಿ ತಿಳಿಸಿದರು.

ಆಸ್ಪತ್ರೆಯ ಶವಾಗಾರಕ್ಕೆ ಹೊಂದಿಕೊಂಡಂತೆ ಇರುವ ಸಿಟಿ ಮಾರುಕಟ್ಟೆಯಲ್ಲಿ ಬಿಸಾಡುವ ಕೊಳೆತ ತರಕಾರಿಯ ದುರ್ವಾಸನೆ ಆಸ್ಪತ್ರೆಗೂ ಹಬ್ಬಿ ನೈರ್ಮಲ್ಯ ಕಾಪಾಡಲು ಸಾಧ್ಯವಾಗುತ್ತಿಲ್ಲ. ಕೊಳೆತ ತರಕಾರಿಗಳನ್ನು ಬೇರೆಡೆ ಸಾಗಿಸುವಂತೆ ಪಾಲಿಕೆ ಆಯುಕ್ತರ ಗಮನಕ್ಕೆ ತರುವುದಾಗಿ ನಫೀಜಾ ಫಜಲ್ ತಿಳಿಸಿಧರು.

ಸಂಜೆವಾಣಿ - 24/10/99

The author on her first visit as Minister of Medical Education of Karnataka incognito to the burns ward of Victoria Hospital in 1999.

Indian Express 18.09.2002

Page- 5

Popularise use of solar energy: Fazal

By Our Staff Correspondent

TUMKUR, SEPT. 18. Nafees Fazal, Minister of State for Science and Technology, said here on Wednesday that the rainwater harvesting scheme, which would be introduced in Bangalore next month, would later be extended to all gram panchayats.

Presiding over the silver jubilee celebration of the Student Project Programme and seminar-cum-exhibition of the Karnataka State Council for Science and Technology at the Siddaganga Institute of Technology, Ms. Fazal said that the scheme was expected to cover 25 per cent of domestic water needs in Bangalore and 50 per cent of the industrial water requirement around the City.

The Government was sorting out the legal aspects by amending the bylaws of the Bangalore Mahanagara Palike, and the scheme would be launched in October.

The Panchayat Raj and Rural Development Department was working on modalities of extending the scheme to all gram panchayats. The Bellandur Gram Panchayat in Bangalore Urban District had come forward to adopt the scheme and it would be developed as a model for other bodies.

Earlier, she visited the house of an engineer, Shivakumar, here to see the adoption of rainwater harvesting technique and the use of solar energy using a simple mechanism.

Stating that a lot of power was consumed for heating water, Ms. Fazal said that efforts should be made to popularise the use solar energy.

She said that the Karnatak University at Dharwad had provided land for setting up a science city there.

The Indian Space Research Organisation (ISRO) had agreed to set up a space museum for which land had been allotted at Bannerghatta in Bangalore.

Praising the council for promoting scientific temper among students, Ms. Fazal said that the Chief Minister, S.M.Krishna, was progressive and modern in his thinking.

He wanted scientific and technological developments to benefit the common man.

The minister said that during her meeting with the President, A.P.J.Abdul Kalam, recently, the latter had stressed on constant interaction between senior scientists and students.

A batch of 15 students had been interacting with scientists at Indian Institute of Science, Bangalore, she said and added that the institute would be requested to continue the exercise.

The Secretary of the council, D.K.Subramanian, and the Principal of the institute, M.N.Channabasappa, spoke.

In the three-day celebrations, students from 30 engineering colleges in the State would present 60 projects at the seminar, and would exhibit 50 chosen projects at the exhibition.

The Vice-Chancellor of Visvesvaraya Technological University, K.Balavera Reddy, will preside over the valedictory function on Friday.

Times Of India
Dt. 3/1/03

While extending a hearty welcome to Hon'ble Prime Minister Sri Atal Behari Vajpayee Karnataka takes yet another pioneering step towards harnessing rain water

Sri Atal Behari Vajpayee
Hon'ble Prime Minister

RAINWATER HARVESTING

The simple, cost-effective solution to recurring water problems.

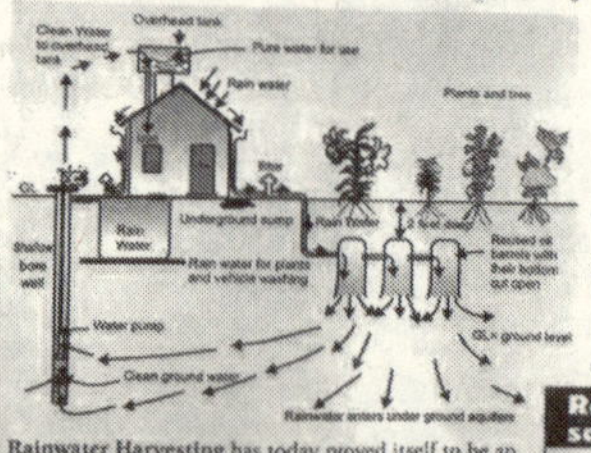

Sri S. M. Krishna
Hon'ble Chief Minister of Karnataka

Smt. Nafees Fazal

...vernment of Karnataka over the ...t three years has done pioneering ...rk in this field. Some of the major ...ps taken by the Government include:

...Amendment of Bangalore Mahanagara Palike Bye-Laws (Clause No.31 of Article 436) has made Rainwater Harvesting mandatory for Multi-storied Apartments, Commercial Complexes and Flats / Buildings with an area of 300 sq.mts and above.

...everal Panchayats have already embarked on ...rticipative Rainwater Harvesting practices

...Department of Science & Technology has initiated ...process of educating Bankers, Farmers, Architects, ...lders and Developers and the general public ...ncrease awareness about Rainwater Harvesting ...its many benefits.

Rainwater Harvesting has today proved itself to be an effective technique of conserving water by guiding the rain water that falls on rooftops to storage tanks or underground sumps for future usage. **Groundwater Recharging**, on the other hand, is undertaken by guiding water through pipes to wells, borewells or recharge pits to ensure recharging water in the underground aquifers, for later use, whenever the need arises.

Come & learn more about this phenomenon at the 'Karnataka Pavilion' at SCIENCE EXPO 2003 during 90th Indian Science Congress from 3rd to 7th January at Jnana Bharati Campus, Sports Ground, Bangalore University, Kengeri.

Rainwater Harvesting saves water and...

- Improves soil moisture
- Increases groundwater level
- Improves the quality of water
- Allows drought-proofing
- Prevents flooding of storm water drains
- Saves energy required to lift water

Department of Science and Technology

karnataka information

Harvest Rain Water - Host a bunch of benefits

The author, as Minister of State for Science and Technology, initiated many projects and schemes to popularise rainwater harvesting. Karnataka was the first state to pioneer rainwater harvesting and solar energy.

Index